TALZOYA

The Traits of Powerful People

Contents

Preface

Fundamentally, power is about access to resources which are essential to survival and reproduction. Within a social context, scarcity creates asymmetry with respect to access to those resources, and asymmetric control over valued resources creates power differentials among the individuals. Differences in power have such a profound influence on outward human behavior that the powerful and the powerless seem to live side by side in different worlds. Having easy access to valued resources makes the powerful less dependent on others, freeing them to act in more self-serving ways. An excess of resources means that they can afford to take greater risks to, potentially, reap greater rewards. Unconstrained by the judgement of others, they can afford to be their authentic selves and live life on their own terms. Hence, they are more likely to experience positive moods, pay attention to social rewards, make quick decisions, and act in uninhibited ways. The powerless, on the other hand, need to serve others in order to access valued resources and are, therefore, forced to act in prosocial ways. Lacking resources means that they have to make more conservative choices and pay close attention to what others want, lest they be punished. Constrained by the threats of others, they are forced to hide their true selves and live life on terms that the powerful dictate. This means that they are more likely to experience negative emotions, pay more attention to threats than to rewards, and behave in more inhibited ways.

Power is intricately related to the notion of control. Even the most challenging circumstances can be more bearable if we feel that we have some say in the outcome, while small stresses may become overwhelming if we feel that we are completely helpless to change the situation. Power differentials are at the root of many mental illnesses. At one end of the extreme, there is the ruthless—and, sometimes, dangerous or violent—pursuit of power observed in those afflicted by mania. On the other end of the extreme, there is the feeling of hopelessness caused by a perceived lack of control over one's life—whether at work or in personal relationships—felt by those suffering from illnesses such as depression and anxiety. Powerlessness can—quite literally—kill. It can wreak havoc on the lives of people who sit low on the totem pole of any social structure, harming not just their mental health, but their physical well-being as well. Lack of control and predictability, lack of coping outlets, and little room for optimism will give free reign to the corrosive effects of chronic stress, which can lead to ill health and a shortened lifespan. Arguably, the biggest predictor of one's health is one's wealth. Study after study has shown that those at the top of the class pyramid live on average longer, healthier lives than the rest of the population. The middle classes fare worse than those on the top, while the poor get sick more often and die sooner. Given these sobering facts, why should everyone not be treated equally? Because despite their negative consequences for some people, power differentials are indispensable to the survival of a social species.

An innate preference for a hierarchical organization is pervasive and universal among all social species, including humans. Hierarchy involves a ranking of individuals along the power spectrum, and power confers the ability to assert the will of those at the top of the social pyramid and *get things done.* Power unleashes the potential of the masses by directing them toward the accomplishment of highly complex purposes that require the coordinated effort of many individuals with varying talents and contributions. Those with the most power—whether it be in the form of money, knowledge, or interpersonal resources—will be the most prominent figures in the political, social, and economic environment. People acting in concert, cooperating, coordinating, and unifying their actions, are able to have an impact on both the physical and social worlds through their interrelatedness that would be impossible if they were solely acting as individual beings. The ensuing rewards benefit everyone in the group, including those at the very bottom of the social ladder. Otherwise stated, hierarchy, obedience to authority, and social order make everyone's life better than it would be if anarchy reigned.

Therefore, power and status matter to *every* individual within a social group. In fact, they matter so much that children, who are just one year of age, can recognize that dominance achieves a *stable* position of power, which is the basis of social hierarchy. Observers studying a group of children can easily detect linear ranks, even as early as between the ages one and two, suggesting that these toddlers are capable of detecting relative status and behave accordingly in dominant or submissive ways when interacting with others. Those occupying the highest ranks in the adult realm are the rich and famous of the world. Power and fame often go hand in hand. In a poll conducted in the United Kingdom by *The Independent* just before Christmas 2006, "being famous" topped the list of what 2,500 children under the age of ten believed to be "the very best thing in the world" (followed by "good looks" and "being rich" at numbers two and three on the list). And among adults, though not all will come out and say it, many have made their life purpose to become famous. Besides satisfying a deep psychological need to be approved by people—comparable to our need for food, water, or shelter—fame provides social proof that we excel at something. Pragmatically, our opportunities are often dictated by others. Indeed, it does not matter if you have written the next great American novel if no one has read it. If you are good at something, you usually need to have it be known that you are good at it. Fame ultimately means expert and referent power, which often bring forth wealth afforded by lucrative commercial endorsement contracts or other business deals. Wealth, in turn, means the ability to live life on your own terms, help others in meaningful ways, and have an impact in the world. Additionally, lasting fame can provide a sense of continuance beyond death—or immortality—and a widely validated sense of self-worth. It signifies exerting power from the grave—this could mean that we all want power, even beyond death.

If power is so important, what is the basis of power? How is social rank bestowed and taken away? How do myriad individuals converge on who deserves the highest ranks and who the lowest ones? Does power corrupt? Are there specific inborn traits that automatically confer power? Are those who strive most ruthlessly for power different, at a biological level, from the rest of the population? Are there character traits that make us more likely to gain power? Are certain behavioral choices more conducive to the attainment of power than others? These are all questions that we will be exploring in this book. So stay focused and enjoy the reading!

Acknowledgement

I want to thank my editor, Andrew Yackira, for his thorough work and professionalism.

I

The Case for Power

1

Living Is Yearning for Power

Power is in need of redemption. Pervasive ignorance drives its general reputation for being corruptive, immoral, or simply evil. Factually, power is nothing more than a tool and, as such, it is fundamentally neutral. Fire, for instance, is a tool that can be used to heat a house for the purpose of protecting its inhabitants from inclement weather, or it can be used to burn down a house for the purpose of killing its inhabitants. The fact that it was used to help life in the first instance and to destroy life in the second does not make it intrinsically good or bad. Its possible use as a weapon of destruction takes nothing away from the instrumental role that the control of fire has played in human evolution. Power can similarly be used with very divergent aims. The fact that it can sometimes be abused does not mean that we should not be seeking or using it. As Gene Simmons puts it, "So much of our popular mythology focuses on the negative aspects of power that we forget that gaining power is, perhaps, the only way to enable ourselves to make a difference in our lives and in the lives of others. . . . The man who gives away his only dollar is a virtuous soul indeed. But when compared to the rich and powerful CEO who gives away 500 million dollars of her five billion dollars, he is not making much of a difference, no matter how noble his intentions. . . . Power moves mountains when mountains need to be moved." The pursuit of power is our natural right and our strongest instinct subserving our basic evolutionary drives to survive and reproduce.

More generally, every living organism is naturally built to seek control over the resources that are critical for its survival and reproduction, or to vie for what we call *power*. This yearning for power, or "will to power"—to borrow a term coined by Friedrich Nietzsche—extends to dominating our physical, biological, and social environments. Across species, social groups are formed for the purpose of exerting power over the environment in a more effective way, compared to acting alone. These groups are known to rapidly self-organize into hierarchies, where high-power members enjoy more food, mates, influence, and other advantages than low-power members. Status, or the group consensus on the pecking order for any given individual, is assigned via a ranking system whereby individuals with either the most desirable traits to be passed onto offspring or the most valuable skills to ensure the group's survival are assigned the highest ranks. Individuals can also influence their status by displaying behaviors or personality traits that reflect dominance, which can be construed as the ability to acquire resources. Generally, power can be gained through aggressive, dominant behaviors, or through prosocial, cooperative actions. Over time such actions can lead to the acquisition of prestige or fame—meaning the widespread recognition of extremely high status—which, in turn, will lessen the need for overt displays of dominance to gain access to valued resources, since others will yield voluntarily. Group consensus, or reputation, is especially important in influencing rank among humans as an alternative to direct observation of valued traits. Hierarchies tend to be pyramid-shaped with few individuals assigned to the highest ranks and large numbers of subordinates at the bottom. The prevalence of hierarchies and their similarities across species suggest a strong innate preference and an evolutionary imperative for the differentiation of power within groups. It also implies an innate ability of individuals across species to rapidly perceive status cues in oneself and others—and to instinctively behave in a dominant or submissive way during interactions with others.

Why would one ever want to voluntarily submit to another? One answer is that doing so reduces the costs of direct aggression to both individuals and minimizes conflict within the group. The cohesion and success of the group profoundly matters to individuals because of the many benefits they derive from it regardless of their power status. These benefits can be in the form of material assets (such as food and shelter) or psychological benefits (such as a sense of security and belongingness). According to research results published in 2015 by Jessica Koski and her collaborators, despite some cross-species variability, there is strong evidence that hierarchies arise out of necessity and that their existence is beneficial to social groups. When essential resources are limited, individual skills vary, and reproductive fitness determines survival, hierarchies are an efficient way to divide goods and labor among group members. Accomplishing complex and risky tasks, such as hunting for big game in our ancestral hunter-gatherer communities, often requires clear division of labor and high levels of coordination among multiple individuals of varying abilities or skills. According to researchers Nir Halevy, Eileen Chou, and Adam Galinsky, within more sophisticated social groups, hierarchy contributes to the formation of a governance structure—explicitly or implicitly—that promotes direction and deference, allowing for concerted, coordinated, and efficient action. In humans, hierarchies fulfill certain fundamental psychological needs better than egalitarian social arrangements—namely, the need for power and achievement and the need for certainty, predictability, and structure. Hierarchies allow fulfillment of the need for certainty, predictability, and structure by establishing a clear chain of command and spheres of authority, as well as corresponding expectations concerning who reports to whom about what, when, and how. Hierarchies can fulfill the need for power and achievement by conditioning rewards and providing opportunities for advancement. Thus, they validate individual beliefs in meritocracy and social mobility, consistent with the preference for equity over equality as a fair and just resource allocation. The perception of fairness and social justice can instill legitimacy into the system, which, in turn, promotes voluntary deference and cooperation. Additionally, in favor of the overall well-being of the group, the advantages and the prestige afforded to higher-ranking members may serve as powerful motivating factors for the rest of the individuals, resulting in an increase in both productivity and creativity of the group as a whole. Finally, hierarchies encourage everyone to defer to the individuals who possess a skill or trait valued by the group, which may be an adaptive component of social learning. Paying attention to successful individuals allows us to imitate their behaviors in the hope of learning a valuable skill from them and, perhaps, achieving our own success. Hence, assigning prestige to certain individuals is a way to lessen confusion and make it clear to everyone in the group who they should preferably observe and emulate. This idea is no better expressed than by Niccolò Machiavelli himself as he advises that, "A prudent man should always follow in the path trodden by great men and imitate those who are most excellent, so that if he does not attain to their greatness, at any rate he will get some tinge of it."

While offering many benefits, group living can sometimes inflict exorbitant costs to the individual. Indeed, successful group action almost always requires coordination, cooperation, and, oftentimes, the willingness to sacrifice oneself for the benefit of the group. For most of human history and prehistory, men, for instance, were expected to be willing to die in war to grow their ruler's (hence, their country's or tribe's) power, while women had to be willing to die in childbirth in order to supply their nation or tribe with additional members. As a general rule, human groups have always sought ways to curb vices, meaning selfish behaviors, and harness virtues, meaning prosocial behaviors. How badly must human beings feel the need to be integrated within groups so as to be willing to voluntarily give up their personal freedom and, sometimes, their lives for the benefit of the group? To appreciate the imperative of socialization for the proper development of a human being, consider the case of Victor of Aveyron, the feral child who was found wandering in the woods near Saint-Sernin-sur-Rance in France in the year 1800. According to Jean-Marc Gaspard Itard, the young physician who eventually adopted him and gave him his name, Victor was a normal child at birth, but was neglected by his alcoholic parents from an early age. Subsequently, around age four or five, he left civilization and fended for himself in the wild for about seven years before being found around age twelve. At the time that he was found, Victor could not speak, and his movements were chaotic. He was soon taken to the National Institute of the

Deaf (despite being capable of hearing) for the purpose of being studied by the renowned priest and instructor of the deaf Roch-Ambroise Cocurron Sicard. Even though he was exposed to society and education over the course of several years that he spent at the institute, Victor made little progress under Sicard. After Sicard became frustrated with the lack of progress made by the boy, he was left to roam the institution by himself, until Itard decided to take the boy into his home to monitor and record details about his development. Despite Itard's efforts spanning many years to civilize Victor, with the objective being to teach him to speak and communicate human emotion, he neither learned to speak beyond a very rudimentary level, nor to display much in the way of basic social behaviors or emotions. Based on the best documented cases of feral children, despite Herculean efforts to teach them, most of them seem to be mentally impaired beyond help; have almost insurmountable trouble learning human language, the basics of hygiene, or learning to walk upright after walking on fours all their lives; and display an almost complete lack of interest in the human activity around them. It seems clear from all this that there is no such thing as a "noble savage." Instead, Thomas Hobbes may have been on the money when he asserted in the *Leviathan* that life in a state of nature is "solitary, poor, nasty, brutish, and short," a "war of all against all." It appears that, unless activated by normal social interactions at an early age, the language and social modules of our brains fail to ever develop much beyond their skeletal forms. The complex social system of coordinated specialized roles in which we all live is what allows us to maintain and expand the vast amount of knowledge that humanity has accumulated. Civilization is what enables us to grow and flourish, while nature shrinks us back to the level of the lower animals. And civilization represents nothing but the apex of collective human power over the environment at any given moment in time. Because Hobbes advocated for absolute monarchy in his *Leviathan*, his vision of the human depravity in a state of nature inspired fervent disagreement among those who opposed absolute government in the seventeenth century. The romantic myth of the noble savage seems to have originated from Shaftesbury, one of Hobbes's prominent opponents, who contended that, contrary to Hobbes's view, humans in a state of nature possessed a moral sense based on the emotion of sympathy and that this emotion was the source and foundation of human goodness and benevolence. In *Soliloquy: Or, Advice for an Author*, he urged a would-be author "to search for that simplicity of manners and innocence of behavior, which has been often known among mere savages; ere they were corrupted by our commerce." This myth was then further perpetuated during the Age of Enlightenment in the late seventeenth and eighteenth centuries which saw opposition to monarchy intensify.

In hindsight, all these beliefs are nonsense: our sympathy and moral sense are encased within the social modules of our brain and can only be activated through complex socialization from a young age. Much of this development seems to be powered by the human brain's natural eagerness for imitation and memorization upon simply being surrounded by other human beings. Hobbes also thought that the absolute rule of a king was the only possible alternative to the otherwise inevitable violence and disorder of civil war. He further argued that the state was founded on a social contract, in which humans voluntarily gave up their liberty in return for the peace and security provided by total surrender to an absolute ruler, whose legitimacy stemmed from the social contract and not from God. Notwithstanding the anachronistic elements in this view, the truth remains that our general tendency for group conformity is exceedingly strong, and our willingness to bend to authority universal and innate.

Exactly how strong is the human willingness to submit to authority? Answering this question quantitatively was especially pertinent in light of the "obedience to authority" defense used by those accused of genocide at the Nuremberg trials after World War II. Was the eagerness to obey authority particularly strong among Germans, or was it universal? If universal, could it be so deeply ingrained in humans as to override human conscience, or moral sense, as well as all training in ethics, sympathy, and moral conduct? From 1933 to 1945 "gas chambers were built, death camps were guarded, daily quotas of corpses were produced with the same efficiency as the manufacture of appliances. These inhumane policies may have originated in the mind of a single person, but they could only be carried out on a massive scale if a very large number of persons obeyed orders." These are some of the thoughts that motivated psychology professor Stanley Milgram at Yale University to start his experiments on obedience to authority in the summer of 1961—about a year after the trial in Jerusalem of Adolf Eichmann, one of the major organizers of the Holocaust.

Milgram and his research team recruited forty male subjects between the ages of twenty and fifty from New Haven, Connecticut, and the surrounding communities via newspaper and direct mail solicitation. The subjects were made to believe that they were to participate in a study of memory and learning at Yale University and offered $4.50 in payment for their willingness to show up, regardless of what happened after they arrived. Subjects ranged in educational level from one who had not finished elementary school to those who had a doctorate and other professional degrees and represented a wide range of occupations form laborers to engineers to business owners. The experiment, repeated forty times (once with each of the forty subjects), consisted in the replay of a scenario comprising three roles: an experimenter, a learner, and a teacher. Each subject showed up at the laboratory at the same time as the learner, who pretended to be another subject responding to the solicitation, but was really a paid actor, a mild-mannered and likable forty-seven-year-old accountant trained for the role. The two participants would then proceed to each draw a slip of paper from a hat to determine whether they would be playing the role of the teacher or that of the learner. The drawing was rigged, as both slips read "teacher"—with the actor always drawing first and lying, reporting that his slip indicated "learner." The experimenter was another actor, a stern- and impassive-looking thirty-one-year-old biology teacher, who wore a grey technician's coat to convey an air of authority. It was expected that the location of the experiment—Yale University, the elegant interaction laboratory on the grounds of an institution of unimpeachable reputation—would induce perceptions of legitimacy in the subjects. Immediately after the drawing, the teacher and learner were taken to an adjacent room by the experimenter, and the learner was strapped into an "electric chair" apparatus. The experimenter explained that the straps were to prevent excessive movement while the learner was being shocked.

The effect was to make it impossible for him to escape from the situation. An electrode was attached to the learner's wrist, and electrode paste was applied "to avoid blisters and burns." Subjects were told that the electrode was attached to the shock generator in the adjoining room. In order to improve credibility, the experimenter declared in response to a question by the learner: "Although the shocks can be extremely painful, they cause no permanent tissue damage." The teacher was then taken to the adjoining electric shock room where he could not see the learner, but could hear him. The lesson to be administered by the teacher was a paired-associate learning task. The teacher read a series of word pairs to the learner, and then read the first word of the pair along with four terms. The learner was to indicate which of the four terms had originally been paired with the first word. He communicated his answer by pressing one of four switches in front of him, which, in turn, lit up one of four numbered quadrants in an answer box located atop the shock generator. The shock generator consisted of thirty lever switches, each of which was clearly labeled from fifteen volts to 450 volts in fifteen-volt increments. In addition, the following verbal designations were clearly indicated for groups of four switches going from left to right: Slight Shock; Moderate Shock; Strong Shock; Very Strong Shock; Intense Shock; Extreme Intensity Shock; Danger: Severe Shock. Details of the instrument were carefully handled to insure an appearance of authenticity. The teacher was told to administer a shock to the learner each time he gave a wrong response and, specifically, to "move one level higher on the shock generator each time the learner flashes a wrong answer." He was also instructed to announce the voltage level before administering a shock so that he would continually be reminded of the increasing intensity of shocks administered to the learner. In all conditions the learner was to give a predetermined set of responses to the word pair test, based on a schedule of approximately three wrong answers to one correct answer. No vocal response or other sign of protest was to be heard from the learner until the 300-volt shock level had been reached. When the 300-volt shock was administered, the learner was to pound on the wall of the room in which he was bound to the electric chair. The pounding could clearly be heard by the teacher. From this point on, the learner's answers no longer appeared on the four-way panel. At this juncture, the teacher would ordinarily turn to the experimenter, who sat in the same room next to him the whole time, for guidance. The experimenter would instruct him to treat the absence of a response as a wrong answer and shock the subject according to the usual schedule. He further advised to allow five to ten seconds before considering no response as a wrong answer and increase the shock level one step each time the learner failed to respond correctly. The learner's pounding was repeated after the 315-volt shock was administered; afterwards he was not heard from, nor did his answers reappear on the four-way signal box. On each occasion that the teacher balked or showed reluctance to follow orders, the experimenter was to give one of four "prods": "Please continue" or "Please go on"; "The experiment requires that you continue"; "It is absolutely essential that you continue"; and "You have no other choice, you must go on." The prods were always made in sequence: only if the first prod had been unsuccessful, could the second prod be used. If the teacher refused to obey the experimenter after the fourth prod, the experiment was terminated. The experimenter's tone of voice was to be firm, but polite. A subject who broke off the experiment at any point prior to administering the thirtieth shock level (or 450 volts) was termed a *defiant* subject. One who complied with experimental commands fully and proceeded to administer all shock levels commanded was termed an *obedient* subject. Unbeknownst to the subjects, Milgram's team tape-recorded the entire experiment, took photographs through one-way mirrors, and took notes on any unusual behavior occurring during the course of the experiment.

Before the experiment occurred, the conditions for it were described to fourteen Yale psychology students in their senior year, and they were asked to predict the likelihood that subjects would be obedient. Their estimate was that 1 percent to 3 percent would obey. When Milgram informally posed the same question to some of his colleagues, the general feeling was that few if any subjects would go beyond the Very Strong Shock designation.

During the experiment, when high voltage levels were reached, subjects were observed to sweat, tremble, stutter, bite their lips, groan, and dig their fingernails into their flesh. Fourteen of the forty subjects showed definite signs of nervous laughter and smiling. The laughter seemed entirely out of place, even bizarre. Full-blown, uncontrollable seizures were observed for three subjects. On one occasion the team observed a seizure so violently convulsive that it was necessary to call a halt to the experiment. No subject stopped, however, prior to administering the 300-volt level, when the victim kicked on the wall and no longer provided answers to the teacher's multiple-choice questions. Of the forty subjects, twenty-six (or 65 percent) were fully obedient, meaning they went all the way to administering the highest voltage of 450 volts. Only fourteen (or 35 percent) stopped between 300 and the highest voltage.

Here is what Milgram had to say about these results in his 1963 publication about the experiment: "Subjects have learned from childhood that it is a fundamental breach of moral conduct to hurt another person against his will. Yet, twenty-six subjects abandon this tenet in following the instructions of an authority, who has no special powers to enforce his commands. To disobey would bring no material loss to the subject; no punishment would ensue. It is clear from the remarks and outward behavior of many participants that, in punishing the victim, they are often acting against their own values. Subjects often expressed deep disapproval of shocking a man in the face of his objections and others denounced it as stupid and senseless. Yet the majority complied with the experimental commands." One has to also note how seriously the Yale University students and professors questioned prior to the experiment underestimated the subjects' willingness to follow the orders of the experimenter to the end. The experiment was repeated by Milgram eighteen more times over the next decade with varying experimental conditions and, also, internationally. The average percentage of fully obedient subjects in both the United States and international experiments roughly concurred with the result of the first Milgram study. It turns out that our innate tendency to obey those whom we perceive to be legitimate authorities trumps, more often than not, our other deeply ingrained disposition not to harm other people—contrary to what most of us would naively assume.

Before anyone rushes to declare obedience to authority evil, it may be important to remember that the very life of society is predicated on its existence. Without it, we would be left to live in absolute chaos. Obedience, just like power, is a neutral tool that can be used for acts of charity and kindness, as well as for acts of destruction. What the Milgram experiments showed was that obedience was the norm among humans, rather than the exception. Obedience to authority is the only way to harness the power of the masses. Absolute deference to the general's orders is necessary if an army wants to have a shot at winning a war. Following the path set by the CEO is the only way for a large corporation to achieve commercial success. As Machiavelli put it, "A crowd is useless without a head." In this sense, it behooves all of us to know who represents the head, and where everyone else stands in relation to it. This may be clearly established through assigned roles and titles in highly structured groups, such as an army or a corporation. But where does the spontaneous emergence of hierarchies within more informal groups, such as a group of children on the playground, stem from? In high schools throughout the world, while some teenagers enjoy great popularity, others are subjected to cruel bullying. How did the students converge on who was popular and who the underdog? Such informal hierarchies can only emerge if, starting from an early age, humans are equipped with mechanisms for rapidly perceiving status information in others and recognizing their relative standing in a group.

Among the visual cues used to assign social rank, body size is the most prominent across the animal kingdom—and this includes humans. Ten-to thirteen-month-old infants can recognize when two novel agents have conflicting goals and predict the winner of the dominance contest between them based on their relative body size. Around one year of age, children recognize that dominance achieves a *stable* position of power, which is the basis of social hierarchy. Observers can easily detect linear rank in groups of children aged one to two years old in real-life situations, suggesting that these toddlers are capable of detecting relative status and behaving in dominant or submissive ways when interacting with others. Even preschool-aged children are able to infer dominance, not only from physical supremacy, but

13

also from decision-making power, age, and resources. Children aged four to five show a preference for interacting with high-status members of the group. Dominant members are also more often watched and imitated than their less-dominant peers, similar to what is observed in primate groups. By the time they enter elementary school, children rapidly form dominance hierarchies which remain stable throughout the school year. Indeed, they are even able to name the popular children who enjoy high status among them. Popularity only grows in importance by early adolescence. Teens have a larger repertoire of cues by which they assess popularity: assigned status increases with height, upper-body strength, age, maturity, masculine-coded facial features in both males and females (indicating a preference for higher levels of testosterone), sexual attractiveness, and intelligence. There is also a strong preference for behaviors indicative of dominance. This can be *aggressive dominance*—exhibiting eye contact while listening, assertiveness, open and expanded body posture during interactions with others, deceitfulness, evasiveness, interrupting others, threatening or bullying others, breaking rules, and persuasiveness—or *sociable dominance*—maintaining eye contact while speaking, acting confidently and generously with others, joining social clubs and making friends, and demonstrating competence, knowledge, or skills. These popularity cues are also used by adults, who additionally incorporate information about someone's income, job title, educational attainment, talent, expertise, influence, number of connections, wealth, and health into their judgements about relative status. The inevitable conclusion from all this is that power matters to all of us. Whether we like admit it or not, we unconsciously judge others and others judge us in all situations from infancy into old age. Short of dying, there is no escaping it. The amount of power we have on our physical and social environment, in turn, influences our well-being, both physical and mental, and fundamentally affects our mood, perception of the world, thoughts, and behavior.

According to research done by Dacher Keltner, Deborah Gruenfeld, and Cameron Anderson in 2003, elevated power is associated with increased rewards and freedom and, thereby, activates approach-related tendencies. Having reduced power is associated with increased threat, punishment, and social constraint and, thereby, activates inhibition-related tendencies. Our behavioral approach system regulates behavior related to sex, food, safety, achievement, aggression, and social attachment. Rewards and opportunities trigger mental processes that help us pursue and obtain goals related to these rewards. Our behavioral inhibition system is equivalent to an alarm-threat system. Inhibition is activated by punishment, threat, and uncertainty. The behavioral inhibition system involves affective states such as anxiety, heightened vigilance, inspection of punishment contingencies, avoidance, and response inhibition. Elevated power activates approach-related processes for two reasons. First, powerful individuals live in environments with abundant resources, including money, food, physical comforts, beauty, and health, as well as social resources, such as flattery, esteem, influence, attraction, and praise. Second, the experience of power involves the awareness that one can act at will without interference or serious social consequences. Acting within reward-rich environments and being unconstrained by the evaluations of others or the consequences of one's actions, people with elevated power are disposed to elevated levels of approach-related affect, cognition, and behavior, including disinhibited sexual behavior and riskier undertakings. Being generally uninhibited, one would also expect their behavior to be a more accurate reflection of their true feelings and personalities. Power confers us the freedom to be our true selves regardless of circumstances and autonomy over our own lives.

In other words, power does not corrupt or make people bad; it just reveals their true nature, be it prosocial or antisocial.

Powerful people tend to construe others through a lens of self-interest. They are quicker to detect opportunities for rewards, such as food, social attention, sex, and money. They tend to treat low-status people in terms of how the latter enable them to satisfy their own personal goals and desires. Since they pay less attention to others generally, they also tend to stereotype more often and judge the attitudes, interests, and positions of others less accurately. They speak up more in public debate and tend to be more actively and physically engaged in group projects. They break rules more often and favor independence.

For complementary reasons, the lack of power is associated with increased inhibition. Powerless individuals have less access to material, social, and cultural resources and are more subject to social threats and punishments. Thus, they are more sensitive to the evaluations and potential constraints of more powerful people. For example, less powerful individuals are more likely to be victims of aggression. This is evident in childhood bullying, which is directed at low-status children, in racism and discrimination against minority groups, in violence against women, and in violent crime perpetrated against members of the lower social classes. Acting in environments with increased punishment, threat, and a lack of resources and being aware of social constraints, people with reduced power are disposed to elevated levels of inhibition-related affect, cognition, and behavior. Being generally inhibited, one would also expect their behavior to less accurately reflect their true feelings and personalities. In short, lack of power reduces our freedom and forces us to adapt our personalities to circumstances and to other people's wills—and, as a consequence, to be less authentic.

In other words, poverty and the lack of power do not ennoble anyone—they just mask their true nature, be it prosocial or antisocial.

Low-power individuals tend to construe themselves with respect to the interests of others and perceive themselves as a means to the ends of high-power individuals. They tend to more carefully scrutinize the actions of others and concentrate their gaze more on others—particularly, those of elevated status. Thus, they are more accurate in judging the attitudes, interests, and positions of others. They speak out less in public debate and are more often passive and withdrawn in group projects. They tend to follow rules and display more dependent tendencies.

Finally, since positive affect facilitates the pursuit of approach-related goals, power will also be associated with increased positive mood. Powerful people experience positive emotions—such as self-confidence, enthusiasm, happiness, hope, or love—more often than less powerful people. In contrast, inhibition is associated with negative mood. Powerless people experience negative emotions—such as self-doubt, guilt, hopelessness, embarrassment, or shame—more often than powerful people. Indeed, members of minority groups and women, both of whom have historically enjoyed less power, often report increased anxiety and depression relative to white males. It would seem, therefore, that high- and low-power individuals inhabit and, through their own actions, create strikingly different worlds—even though they live side by side. Since group living is such an existential part of a human life and given that groups tend to favor hierarchies, it behooves us to better understand the concept of *influence*, or *social power*—meaning the ability of high-power members to induce a change in the behavior, opinions, attitudes, goals, needs, values, thoughts, and emotions of low-power members.

For any given individual to motivate a change in another, the latter must perceive a quality in the first to justify the change. John French, Jr. and Bertram Raven have identified five bases of social power (to which Raven later added a sixth basis). These six bases of power are:

1. *Reward power*, based on the ability to mediate rewards.
2. *Coercive power*, based on the ability to mediate punishments or costs.
3. *Legitimate power*, based on the perception that one has a right—assigned by group consensus—to prescribe behaviors.
4. *Referent power*, on the basis of others' willingness to identify and affiliate with a particular individual.
5. *Expert power*, based on the perception that one has some special knowledge or expertise.
6. *Informational power*, based on the belief that one is in possession of valuable information.

Reward power is all about being in a position to reward others for compliance with one's wishes and directives. A work supervisor, for instance, can award bonuses, pay raises, promotions, or extra time off to her subordinates for timely and successful completion of projects. The draw of reward, or positive reinforcement, can foster healthy competition, which can increase excitement, productivity, learning, and creativity across the team. The strength of the reward power increases with the magnitude of the rewards one can mediate and the perceived probability that one can effectively bestow the rewards. For example, supervisors rarely have complete control over salary increases and, often, managers cannot control promotions all by themselves. This can affect the level of compliance that they can achieve among subordinates. Another frustration of using rewards is that they often need to be bigger each time if they are to have the same motivational impact. Even then, if rewards are given frequently, people can become satiated, resulting in a loss of effectiveness and decreased power for the power holder. Uneven rewards can also stoke envy and jealousy within a team and lead to unhealthy competition, resulting in dysfunctional team dynamics. Rewards are not limited to those that one can bestow in the workplace—they can be as diverse as affection, friendship, sexual favors, care, food, shelter, advice, or praise. Social groups, for instance, often condition acceptance into the group upon conformity to group norms. Their power is based upon the belief that the benefits of group membership outweigh the cost of compliance.

Coercive power stems from the ability to inflict punishments for noncompliance. A supervisor can convey this type of power by instilling in his or her subordinates the fear of losing their job, being demoted, receiving a poor performance review, or having projects taken away for poor performance. The strength of the coercive power increases with the magnitude of the punishments one can inflict and the perceived probability that compliance will avoid the punishment. Continuous use of threats often builds resentment and resistance from the people who experience it. This resentment is the very source of the bad reputation that power generally has, as coercion has traditionally been the preferred method of exerting power. In the corporate world, if employees fear being punished for every instance of failure, they will be strongly incentivized to be as conservative as possible in every endeavor and abstain from innovation, which often comes at the price of frequent failures. Additionally, when something goes wrong, employees will have a strong incentive to keep it hidden, which can worsen the situation over time. Other examples of coercive power include the use of physical violence to inflict biological harm, verbal violence to inflict psychological harm, and malicious rumors to damage someone's reputation or standing within a group. Nations can threaten individuals with imprisonment or fines for failure to obey their laws. More informal groups can also threaten members with banishment for noncompliance with group norms.

Legitimate power arises from group consensus, which dictates that some members have a special right to influence others, who, in turn, have the obligation to accept this influence. Group consensus is tacit (or informal) when reflected in generally accepted norms, and explicit (or formal) when written into laws, codes of conduct, or job descriptions. Tacit group norms and customs are usually taught from an early age, which allows them to become internalized and gain the strength of instincts. Legitimate power is very similar to the notion of legitimacy of authority. It involves some sort of code or standard, accepted by the individual, by virtue of which the external agent can assert his or her power. Cultural values, such as age, intelligence, social class, gender, and other physical characteristics, constitute one common basis for the legitimate power of one individual over another. This basis of legitimate power is often discriminatory, and it is, therefore, increasingly being challenged in the modern world. Legitimate power in a formal organization is largely a relationship between offices rather than between persons. And the acceptance of an office as right is a basis for legitimate power. For example, a CEO is granted the authority to determine the overall direction and resource needs of a company; a judge has a right to levy fines; a foreman assigns work; a priest prescribes religious beliefs; and it is the management's prerogative to make certain decisions. The election of a representative to political office is, perhaps, the most common example of a group's serving to legitimize the authority of one individual or office for other individuals in the group. Use of legitimate power is typically restricted to a specified range—for example, the activities specified within a supervisory role's job description. The attempted use of legitimate power which is outside of its range will decrease the power of the authority figure. Past cultures have afforded especially broad power for certain groups over others. In many cultures, men were broadly granted the right to prescribe the behavior of women in all situations, and upper-class members were given broad discretion in their treatment of those in the lower social classes. This type of power can have an especially detrimental effect on the targeted individuals, who, being born subjected to it, have usually come to internalize its legitimacy from a young age, entrapped in a perpetual cycle of increasing powerlessness. In many modern cultures, these practices have largely been deemed unjust and, fortunately, have become unlawful acts.

Referent power stems from the desire to identify or become closely associated or affiliated with a person or group one perceives to be attractive. A person may be admired because of specific personal traits or talents, and this admiration creates the opportunity for interpersonal influence. In order to establish an affiliation and maintain it, the lower-status person will behave, believe, and perceive as the admired person does. Celebrities often hold great referent power over their fans. Advertisers have long used the referent power of sports figures for product endorsements. The charismatic appeal of the sports star leads to an acceptance of the endorsement, although the individual may have little real credibility outside the sports arena. If the respected entity is a group, then the lower-status person will have a feeling of membership or a desire to join the group. Nationalism and patriotism are examples of such referent power. The wish to attend Ivy League universities stems from a desire to be affiliated with their prestige and personally benefit from their positive aura in the workplace. The degree of referent power increases with the strength of the attraction the power holder elicits in others. Referent power stems, in all likelihood, from the innate propensity among humans and other social animals to imitate individuals perceived to be prestigious with the end goals of learning something valuable from them and achieving success in their own turn.

Expert power comes from one's experiences, knowledge, talents, or skills. When individuals demonstrate knowledge and skills that enable them to understand a situation, suggest solutions, use solid judgment, and generally outperform others, then people tend to listen to them, trust and respect them, and follow their recommendations. Accepting an attorney's advice in legal matters or a doctor's medical advice in matters of health are common examples of expert influence. University professors tend to be respected members of society, as they are believed to have a great deal of knowledge in their specialized fields. A native villager can give a stranger directions which the stranger will accept, and this trust is based on the belief that the villager has extensive experience with the locality. When conformity with majority opinion is based on respect for the collective wisdom of the group, it represents another instance of expert power. It is worth noting that the combination of expert power with creativity and some luck is at the root of all human progress and the means by which humans exert power over their physical and biological environments. This explains why those with a high degree of expert power garner special respect among their admirers. When they can bring about lasting positive change, they join the ranks of those who make history.

Informational power is the ability to bring about change through the resource of information that others need or want (in order to reach an important goal) or simply wish to keep secret (in order to avoid personal damage). Informational power is the most transitory type of power; if one gives information away then the power is given away. When the information is complex, it can confer longer-lasting power: the information holder can give it out in bits and pieces to a target of influence to lay the groundwork for future persuasion. Not all information is readily available. Some information is closely controlled by few people, such as material nonpublic information about a publicly traded company. This can be a double-edged type of power: trading in stocks on the basis of material nonpublic information can make you rich, but, if caught, it can land you in prison for breaching laws established to maintain the integrity of the public securities markets. Being in possession of such information is not the result of any particular expertise, but stems from simply holding a certain job or belonging to a network of people with access to such information. In that sense, informational power is distinct from expert power. It can stem from special access to restricted information or timely access to otherwise public information. Information can, and often is, used as a weapon in certain instances, such as divorce, business dissolution, or in civil suit discoveries. Information can been used to extort action, utterance, agreement, or settlement. Timely and relevant information delivered on demand can be an effectual way to acquire power. How information is used—sharing it with others, limiting it to key people, organizing it, increasing it, or even falsifying it—can create a shift in power within a group.

Powerful people often derive their power from a combination of these six bases of power. A supervisor, for instance, enjoys legitimate power through her job title, but also holds reward and coercion powers to the extent afforded by her job description. If she is particularly respected and admired by her team, she might also have referent power. She was probably elevated to a supervisory role because of specialized knowledge or job experience and, hence, holds some level of expert power. If she is privy to restricted information within the firm, she may have some degree of informational power as well. The level of power she enjoys within her team is probably very different from the power she has in the overall firm. This power can increase or decrease over time. Her level of power in the workplace may also be very different from the power she has at home. Thus, power is always relative to one's circumstances. If individuals differ in the amount of power that they hold, they also differ in the ways that they choose to put their power to use. Abuse, which is based on selfish or callous use, is what gives power its bad reputation of being corruptive. In contrast, many powerful individuals choose to be conspicuously altruistic. But, even when considering some of the most altruistic-looking acts, it is hard to pinpoint where selfishness ends and pure altruism starts.

2

Altruism Is a Way of Gaining Power and, in Truth, Selfishness in Disguise

As we learned in the previous chapter, the implications of achieving high status in one's community or group are profound. Those higher on the social ladder have easier access to scarce resources, receive more social support, enjoy better physical and mental health, better reproductive success, and even a longer life. It is no surprise, then, that the pursuit of status should be pervasive in social groups. According to a 2009 research publication by psychologists Cameron Anderson and Gavin Kilduff, one way that individuals pursue status is by providing or *appearing* to provide value to the group. And what a group values most are traits that help to enhance the survival of the group, even when it comes at the cost of an individual's life. From the perspective of the individual, however, it seems best to attain prestige at the least possible cost to oneself. Interestingly, status is, in fact, awarded based on actual competence and generosity, or the mere appearance of those traits. A cheap way to attain prestige is, therefore, to act confidently (which suggests superior task competence) or to act generously toward others (which suggests a strong commitment to the group). Is it any surprise, then, that the personality trait *dominance*, which involves a preference for possessing authority and the tendency to behave assertively, and individual differences such as the need for power and self-monitoring, which are also associated with a desire for high social standing, are consistently found to be reliable predictors of the actual attainment of higher status in group settings? They are, in fact, better predictors of power status than even intelligence. Dominant individuals can convey superior competence, even when they lack it, by simply showing initiative and conveying confidence in their abilities. Overly positive self-views and behaviors help individuals convince others that they are more capable than they actually are. Individuals pursuing status can also attain it by signaling their commitment to the group through displays of selflessness. The acts of generosity can be relatively small and low-cost; what matters more is to show care consistently and publicly. Indeed, being or appearing to be competent and generous may not be enough; one also has to overcome the barrier of anonymity. Hence, status seekers are keen on enhancing their social standing by developing a wider range of relationships with other group members. Being sociable and socially connected helps to be noticed for one's displays of competence and generosity, which is necessary to enhance one's reputation—hence, status through group consensus. This helps explain why extraverts and those who seek to wield power consistently attain status within larger social groups, as they tend to draw more attention to themselves and develop a wider range of social relationships.

What makes a species social is the willingness of individuals to help others in certain circumstances. The intention to benefit others at a cost to oneself forms the core of what we call *altruism*. Acts of generosity within small kinship groups are frequently observed among many species of mammals. This type of altruism is usually explained by the *kin selection theory*, which posits that organisms can increase their inclusive fitness by contributing to the reproductive success of their relatives, even at a cost to the organism's own survival and reproduction. From a genetic perspective, evolutionary success ultimately depends on leaving behind the maximum number of copies of one's genes in the population. Our own offspring carries one half of our genetic material. Hence, a sibling's child, who will carry one quarter of our genes, is a half-offspring equivalent. Helping a sibling to have and raise children ultimately helps us to propagate some of our own genes, probably at a far smaller cost than having and raising children by ourselves. Hence, the shadow of selfishness already lurks behind the seemingly selfless altruism in kin selection. Additionally, humans have the unique ability among mammals to form and cooperate within large social groups, which include many genetic strangers. For example, humans often invest time and energy in helping other members in their neighborhood, friends, or coworkers. This type of generosity is typically explained via the *reciprocal altruism theory*, which posits that individuals sometimes act in a manner that temporarily reduces their fitness, while increasing another's fitness, with the expectation that the other individual will act in a similar manner at a later time. Ulterior selfishness is apparent in this tit-for-tat strategy; it is all about making a debtor out of someone. In some cases, we may never get any reciprocal help, but in others, we may obtain far more in the future than we gave away ourselves. So long as the sum total of what we get minus the sum total of what we give is positive over the long run, the strategy benefits us. But what exactly motivates humans when they donate to charity, come to each other's rescue in crises and disasters, or respond to appeals to sacrifice for their country during a war? Neither the kin selection theory nor the reciprocal altruism theory seem appropriate in those cases.

In 2006, Charlie Hardy and Mark Van Vugt of the University of Kent at Canterbury came up with a novel theory of altruism called *competitive altruism*, which can account for a range of altruistic behaviors among humans that theories of kinship and reciprocity cannot easily explain. Competitive altruism is the process through which individuals attempt to outcompete each other in terms of generosity. It emerges because altruism enhances the status and reputation of the giver. Status, in turn, yields benefits that would be otherwise unattainable. By spending excessive amounts of energy, time, and money on activities that are essentially unselfish, altruists advertise some desirable underlying quality that is costly to obtain and, therefore, hard to fake, such as resource control, genetic endowment, health, or vigor. This follows from the simple fact that one must have something in order to be able to give something, preferentially in excess amount, especially when the giving is costly. The altruist benefits by increasing his or her social status and, thus, the likelihood that he or she will be preferentially chosen as a mate or business ally in the future. People may be more willing to do business with the altruists than self-centered persons because they trust the former more to look out for the interests of others, including their own. Potential sexual partners may also be willing to mate with them preferentially because they infer from their gift of resources that they possess wealth, which is essential to comfortably raise offspring, but, even more importantly, that they are willing to share their resources. Indeed, a wealthy spouse is not of much use if they are also callous and stingy. Thus, the altruists are able to recoup the short-run costs of their display of generosity in the long run. When reputations are at stake, this is likely to induce competition. On one hand, people will be competing with each other in terms of generosity to advertise themselves as future exchange partners, and on the other hand, observers are competing for access to the most altruistic partners, hence, the term *competitive altruism*.

Competitive altruism can motivate individuals to closely monitor their own behaviors and those of others in social settings. *Self-monitoring* is mostly performed subconsciously and is characterized by an acuteness of perception, discernment, and understanding of social situations and a willingness to regulate one's behavior to accommodate social situations. High self-monitors can accurately identify social structures—the makeup of exchange relations that connect members of their social group. They can be thought of as social pragmatists who project images of themselves in an attempt to impress others and receive positive feedback. In comparison to low self-monitors, high self-monitors participate in more expressive control and have concern for situational appropriateness. As these individuals are willing to adjust their behavior, others may perceive them to be more receptive, pleasant, and benevolent towards them. In a 2006 publication, Francis Flynn and his research collaborators have shown that high self-monitors elevate their social status among their peers by establishing a reputation as generous exchange partners. Specifically, they are more likely than low self-monitors to refrain from asking others for help, while being more frequently sought out for help by their peers. This is because those who assume the role of help-seeker tend to occupy a lower status position—they not only expose themselves to denial and rejection, they also acknowledge their dependence on others. As a result, high self-monitors tend to be perceived as better performers, develop more favorable reputations, and be promoted to higher ranking positions in organizations.

Acts of callousness may make the headlines, but all the media of the world would not be enough to list half the acts of generosity that we each experience in our everyday lives. People are typically not consciously aware of the long-run benefits of altruism. Their generous actions do not usually carry planned ulterior motives; they do not consciously expect their generosity to be repaid in any particular fashion or within any given timeframe, or even to be repaid at all. Humans have enjoyed the long-run benefits of altruism for so long that they have come to behave generously towards others without consciously knowing why they do it. The willingness to act with generosity is, in all likelihood, etched into our brains prenatally and becomes activated when placed in ideal social settings during childhood and adolescence. Being generous toward others makes us feel happy about ourselves, instinctively. Acting with callousness, on the other hand, tends to make us feel guilty and anxious. This follows from a deep understanding that generosity rarely goes unpaid and callousness will quickly tarnish a reputation, causing harm that is very hard to reverse. When specifically asked why they made a charitable donation, donors might simply respond that it made them feel good to do so. But our brain's pleasure centers light up, precisely, to motivate us into taking those actions that enhance our chances at survival and reproduction. Actions that elevate us in social standing are squarely in that category, given that with high status come respect, influence, wealth, better mates, more friends, more comfort, less stress, health, longevity, and ultimately life success.

Activating the neural scaffolding of generosity in a toddler's brain requires timely socialization. The *norm of reciprocity* is one of the earliest of moral precepts taught to children universally. It states that if someone gives something to us, we should feel obligated to repay that debt. Moreover, nearly everyone—with the exception of the young, the sick, and the old—is subject to it. By obligating the recipient to an act of future repayment, the norm of reciprocity allows one person to give something to another with the confidence that it is not being lost. The mutually beneficial exchanges of our ancestors evolved into a sound interdependence among humans that has contributed to our success as a species. As a result, all major religious and ethical traditions include reciprocity as a prime, if not golden, rule of moral behavior. The norm of reciprocity is a social convention that simply compels us to return a favor done to us and respond with either indifference or hostility to harms. Anything taught to us early in life tends to gain the strength of instinct, which is why religious and moral precepts are instilled as early as toddlerhood. A toddler's brain is a bit like a sponge designed mainly to absorb by imitation and memorization. Without the cognitive ability to criticize, it will accept any precept or norm coming from trusted adults. Well-learned and accepted, or *internalized*, norms tend to guide our behavior in an almost reflexive way into adulthood, and even into old age, if left unquestioned. Very few fail to see the value that the norm of reciprocity provides when they question it as adults—because they see it as intrinsically rewarding, they can accept the ideas and behaviors it entails and consciously choose to make it a part of their value system.

The norm of reciprocity is a powerful engine for motivating, creating, sustaining, and regulating the cooperative behavior required for self-sustaining social organizations, controlling the damage done by the unscrupulous and contributing to social system stability. We feel obliged to reciprocate acts of goodwill. We also expect others to repay our own helpful behavior. The expectation that another group member will feel obligated when helped can induce help in the first place, triggering a host of continuing exchanges benefiting each party as debts are honored. Broad systems of trade, division of labor, and protection that emerge from reciprocal exchanges serve group needs as well. Whilst we seek to repay helpful behavior, we sometimes wish to see those who act against our interests punished. The prospect of revenge alone can sometimes deter a harmful act, and this helps to keep balance in social systems. Because this norm is usually internalized, it may induce the sense that following it is an imperative rather than a choice, and failing to reciprocate should create feelings of self-reproach and guilt. According to Mark Whatley and collaborators, another complementary way of understanding how the norm of reciprocity operates is to appreciate that the initial benefit and any subsequent reciprocation almost always unfolds in a public way. And, as with any important social norm, both the social rewards of following the norm and the social costs of violating it can be far-reaching. Most people will want to avoid the shame of an unsavory reputation and the social ruin of ostracism—for most, this is a good enough reason to adhere to the norm. Based on the experiments that Whatley and collaborators conducted in 1999, the norm of reciprocity appears to operate through at least two types of processes. The first type of process could be described as a more private one, in which people respond to a strongly internalized belief that both performing and returning good deeds are the right and proper things to do. The second type seems to be a more public process, in which people respond to the social rewards and costs associated with following or violating this publicly accepted and acclaimed norm.

The norm of reciprocity is often used by marketers to manipulate the behavior of prospective customers. Advertisers routinely design marketing campaigns to offer a sense that a company has helped potential customers in some way so that they may induce an obligation to buy their product or service. As any discerning vacationer at a resort town in Mexico can relay, exhortations to buy into costly (and often financially nonsensical) time-share contracts rely on three automated processes for their success: the halo effect of the good mood induced by the relaxed, sunshiny, and luxurious atmosphere; impulsivity; and the sense of obligation to reciprocate small favors from the marketer (such as a free breakfast, free day trips, or vouchers to a luxurious spa) by the much bigger favor of signing their paperwork and wiring the first of what will turn out to be a long-running series of large payments. Indeed, according to psychologist Robert Cialdini, the norm of reciprocity can trigger unparalleled cognitive dissonance, which often leads to unequal exchanges. This rule also exerts its power by making us feel compelled to overcome our feelings of dislike or suspicion for the person who gives us a gift. This makes it a particularly useful tool for manipulation. For instance, some companies will offer a free trial of their products—such as mattresses or gym equipment—and propose to deliver them to customers' homes for free. These companies will often emphasize to the customers that they can return the product after a specified period of time if they are unhappy with it for any reason. At the end of the trial period, a customer may feel that the product does not meet their needs and want to return it. Then, they realize the effort that the company must put into processing the return. The norm of reciprocity leads them to feel reluctant to inconvenience the company and feel obliged to reciprocate the favor of the free trial by purchasing and keeping the product. Charities also use the norm of reciprocity to solicit donations. They send fundraising requests to previous donors along with a free item, such as a set of stickers or a shiny quarter. As there is no way to return the free gift, donors feel obliged to repay the charities' kindness with a generous donation. These are cases that perfectly befit the adage "there is no such thing as a free lunch." Cialdini emphasizes that we are, however, not powerless to the strength of the norm of reciprocity. Despite the norm's psychological influence, we have the ability to effectively discern, adjust, or simply say *no* to attempts at exploitative reciprocation.

To further appreciate how selfishness and altruism often blend into one another, let's take a look at the deeds of one of the greatest industrialists and philanthropists known: Andrew Carnegie. In one of the most spectacular rags-to-riches ascents, Carnegie rose from his humble beginnings as the child of poor Scottish immigrants to become a tycoon of the steel industry in the late nineteenth century and, then, one of the richest Americans in history by the beginning of the twentieth century. He built Pittsburgh's Carnegie Steel Company, which he sold to J. P. Morgan in 1901 for a little over 300 million dollars (the equivalent of billions of dollars at the time of this writing). The company was renamed U.S. Steel Corporation. After selling Carnegie Steel, he surpassed John D. Rockefeller, the oil industry tycoon, as the richest American for the next several years. In the last eighteen years of his life, he gave away about 350 million dollars—roughly 90 percent of his fortune—to various institutions, with the goal of promoting the arts and sciences, public education, and world peace. His charitable deeds include building Carnegie Hall in New York City, the Peace Palace in the Hague, the Carnegie Institution for Science in Washington, DC, the Carnegie Trust for the Universities of Scotland, the Carnegie Mellon University and the Carnegie Museums of Pittsburgh, and numerous local libraries for general public education, among others. Whilst nobody can deny the immense social benefit of his altruism in old age, Carnegie was a cutthroat businessman throughout his career, with little sympathy for the working classes, including his own employees. He was notorious for using any means available to accumulate wealth and power, including engaging in insider trading and using his political influence to crush competitors. He was a ruthless and talented self-promoter who could have given lessons to Niccolò Machiavelli himself in the art of guarding and enhancing one's public image. Two prominent events that occurred during his career in the steel industry help to shed some light on his character.

The first incident is the Johnstown flood of 1889. The village of Johnstown was founded by Swiss immigrants in Pennsylvania in the year 1800 on the banks of the Conemaugh River. It began to prosper with the building of the Pennsylvania Main Line Canal in 1836 and the construction in the 1850s of the Pennsylvania Railroad and the Cambria Iron Works. By 1889, Johnstown's industries had attracted numerous Welsh and German immigrants. With a population of 30,000 people, it was a growing industrial community known for the quality of its steel. The Conemaugh River flows from high up in the Allegheny Mountains down to the east of Johnstown in the valley, making the town especially prone to flooding, even today. Additionally, slag from the iron furnaces of the steel mills was dumped along the river to create more land for building, which resulted in an artificial narrowing of the riverbed and increased the town's vulnerability to flooding. High above the city, the Commonwealth of Pennsylvania built the South Fork Dam between 1838 and 1853, as part of an interstate canal system. Lake Conemaugh, the reservoir behind the dam, supplied Johnstown with water. As railroads superseded canal barge transport, the Commonwealth abandoned the canal and sold it to the Pennsylvania Railroad. In 1881, Henry Clay Frick, an especially cutthroat—and even violent—businessman led a group of wealthy speculators from Pittsburgh in purchasing the abandoned reservoir, modifying it, and converting it into a private mountain resort lake called South Fork Fishing and Hunting Club. This club, constructed solely for themselves and their wealthy associates, all of whom (along with Frick himself) were connected through business and social links to Carnegie Steel, eventually came to comprise nearly sixty leading business tycoons from Western Pennsylvania. This included Frick and Carnegie themselves, Frick's best friend Andrew Mellon, and Frick's prominent attorneys, Philander Knox and James Hay Reed of Knox and Reed. Shortly after the purchase, the club made the decision to lower the dam by three feet in order to build a road on top of it. Cottages and a clubhouse were built. Additionally, three cast-iron discharge pipes that previously allowed a controlled release of water, which were sold for scrap by a previous owner, were never replaced by the club. Between 1881 and 1889, the dam frequently sprang leaks and was patched cheaply, mostly with mud and straw. On May 30, 1889, a major storm system formed over Johnstown, which dumped six to ten inches of rain over the region in a twenty-four-hour period. During the night, small creeks became roaring torrents, ripping out trees and debris. Telegraph lines were downed, and rail lines were washed away. Before daybreak, the Conemaugh River that ran through Johnstown was about to overwhelm its banks. All morning on May 31, men at the South Fork Fishing and Hunting Club desperately tried to devise ways to unclog spillways, create a new spillway, and even plough earth on top of the dam in desperate efforts to keep the water from gushing down the hill. They sent one man down the hill to warn the people of Johnstown of a possible catastrophic flood. But the warnings were not passed to the authorities in town, as there had been many false alarms of a similar kind in the past. Out of exhaustion and the fear that their efforts were futile and the dam was at risk of imminent collapse, the men up the hill abandoned their efforts by early afternoon and took refuge on higher ground. Shortly afterwards, the dam broke, releasing over fourteen million cubic meters of water down the hill. This was the worst flood to hit the United States in the nineteenth century. In the end, 1,600 homes were destroyed, seventeen million dollars in property damage was levied (nearly half a billion in 2020 dollars), and four square miles of downtown Johnstown were completely destroyed. A total of 2,208 people were killed, a civilian death toll only surpassed in American history by fatalities in the 1900 Galveston hurricane and the September 11, 2001 terrorist attacks. A hydraulic analysis published in 2016 confirmed what had long been suspected: that the changes made to the dam by the South Fork Fishing and Hunting Club severely reduced the ability of the dam to withstand major storms. Lowering the dam and failing to replace the discharge pipes at the base of the dam had cut the safe discharge capacity of the dam by half. The fatal lowering of the dam greatly reduced the capacity of the main spillway and virtually eliminated the action of an emergency spillway on the western abutment. One of the first outsiders to arrive into Johnstown was Clara Barton, nurse, founder, and president of the American Red Cross. Barton arrived on June 5, 1889, to lead the group's first major disaster relief effort; she did not leave for more than five months. Donations for the relief effort came from all over the United States and overseas. In 1889, nearly four million dollars was collected for the Johnstown relief effort from within the United States and eighteen foreign countries. Meanwhile, what did the tycoon members of the South Fork Fishing and Hunting Club contribute? Along with about half of the club members, cofounder Frick offered a donation of merely a few thousand dollars to the relief effort in Johnstown. Later, when lawsuits were filed accusing the club of failing to maintain the dam properly, the club was successfully defended by the firm of Knox and Reed, whose partners Philander Knox and James Hay Reed were both club members. The club was never held legally responsible for the disaster. Knox and Reed successfully argued that the dam's failure was a natural calamity, which was an act of God. Not a cent was paid to the survivors of the flood. Moreover, the members of the club successfully suppressed most bad press related to the incident, refrained from ever mentioning the club or the flood, and actively delayed and whitewashed a report by the committee from the American Society of Civil Engineers sent to investigate the event. What did Andrew Carnegie do to both salvage and enhance his reputation? He built a library for Johnstown after the cleanup (which took several years) and started similar altruistic projects elsewhere—including the 1891 construction of Carnegie Hall, to this day one of the most prestigious venues in the world for both classical and popular music. In all of this, where exactly did his selfishness stop and pure altruism start?

The second incident was the 1892 Homestead Strike. The Homestead Strike was a bloody labor confrontation at Carnegie Steel's main plant in Homestead, Pennsylvania. The strike, one of the most serious in the history of the United States, lasted several months. It grew out of a labor dispute between the Amalgamated Association of Iron and Steel Workers (AA) and the Carnegie Steel Company. In February of 1892, with the steel industry doing well and steel prices higher, the AA, representing 800 of the 3,800 workers at the plant, asked management for a wage increase. The bargaining agreement between the AA and the plant was set to expire on June 30, 1892. Henry Clay Frick, Andrew Carnegie's violently antiunion friend and executive employee since 1881 (the equivalent of today's Chief Operations Officer), immediately countered with an average 22 percent wage decrease that would affect nearly half the union's membership and remove a number of positions from the bargaining unit. Having learnt a valuable lesson in reputation management from the Johnstown flooding incident, what did Andrew Carnegie do when the dispute started to go in the wrong direction? He conveniently left for an extended trip to Scotland just before the unrest peaked, leaving Frick entirely in charge of mediating the clash. In fact, Carnegie specifically instructed Frick to use the negotiations to break the union. As the union and the company failed to come to an agreement, management locked the union out of the plant on June 29. A high fence topped with barbed wire, begun earlier in the year, was completed and the plant sealed to the workers. Sniper towers with searchlights were constructed near each mill building, and high-pressure water cannons (some capable of spraying boiling-hot liquid) were placed at each entrance. Various aspects of the plant were protected, reinforced, or shielded. On June 30, the AA decided to strike. Workers at Carnegie plants in Pittsburgh, Duquesne, Union Mills, and Beaver Falls struck in sympathy the same day. In the following days at Homestead, the strikers were determined to keep the plant closed, not allowing anybody in. Sympathetic townspeople helped them take shifts throughout the day to watch ferries and trains, keep strangers out of town, and monitor the company's attempts to hire replacement workers. Meanwhile, Frick was also busy. The company placed ads for replacement workers in newspapers all over the country, and even in Europe. His intent was to open the works with nonunion men on July 6. In preparation for this, 300 agents working for Pinkerton—a private security guard and detective agency—were hired, equipped with rifles, placed on two specially equipped barges on the Ohio River, and told to tow upriver towards Homestead. Alerted to the move, a small flotilla of union boats went downriver to meet the barges. Strikers on the steam launch fired a few random shots at the barges, then withdrew after blowing the launch whistle to alert the plant. The strikers blew the plant whistle at 2:30 a.m., drawing thousands of men, women, and children to the plant. As the Pinkertons attempted to disembark around 4:00 a.m., more shots were fired, and one man on each side was wounded. The Pinkerton agents aboard the barges then fired into the crowd, killing two and wounding eleven. The crowd responded in kind, killing two and wounding twelve. The Pinkertons attempted to disembark again at 8:00 a.m. A striker high up the riverbank fired a shot. The Pinkertons returned fire, and four more strikers were killed. A few more casualties occurred before the Pinkertons finally surrendered at 5:00 p.m. As the strike continued on in the following days, on July 12 at 9:00 a.m., the Pennsylvania state militia arrived at the small Munhall train station near the Homestead mill. More than 4,000 soldiers surrounded the plant. Within twenty minutes, they had displaced the picketers. By 10:00 a.m., company officials were back in their offices. Another 2,000 troops camped on the high ground overlooking the city. The company quickly brought in strikebreakers and restarted production under the protection of the militia. New employees, many of them black, arrived on July 13, and the mill furnaces relit just two days later. National attention became riveted on Homestead when, on July 23, Alexander Berkman, a New York anarchist with no connection to steel or to organized labor, attempted to assassinate Frick. He came in from New York, gained entrance to Frick's office, then shot and stabbed the executive. Frick survived and continued his role; Berkman was sentenced to twenty-two years in prison. The Berkman assassination attempt undermined public support for the union and prompted the final collapse of the strike. On August 12, the company announced that 1,700 men were working at the mill, and production had resumed at full capacity. The state militia pulled out on October 13. With only 192 out of more than 3,800 strikers in attendance, the Homestead chapter of the AA voted to return to work on November 20, 1892. The Homestead strike broke the AA as a force in the American labor movement. In the end, about 2,500 men lost their jobs at the Homestead plant, and wages were reduced by 50 percent for the remaining workers. Carnegie and Frick had won the bitter battle.

Carnegie's reputation did take a temporary hit following the 1892 incident. True to himself, he kept on with his altruistic projects, which included the founding of the Carnegie Museum of Art in Pittsburgh in 1895. With it, he started to rise again in public opinion. By 1901, since the fortune he had amassed when he sold Carnegie Steel to J. P. Morgan and retired from the steel industry was too enormous for anyone to spend on oneself in a lifetime, he did the next best thing he could do with it—he spent it on public projects that were dear to him. In the process, he built a fabulous legacy to last for centuries to come. To most people's knowledge today, he is one of the greatest industrialists and philanthropists to have ever lived. The details of the Johnstown and Homestead incidents are mostly forgotten or, in any case, rarely mentioned in connection to his name.

Carnegie's deeds constitute a vivid illustration of competitive altruism in action, where one helps others to indirectly help oneself, even from beyond the grave. Note that this fact takes nothing away from the immense public benefit that has resulted from the institutions that he has founded. Whilst he was a cutthroat businessman during his tenure in the steel industry, he still provided employment and wages to tens of thousands of people over the course of a few decades and contributed to progress and efficiency in steel production. From a moral perspective, it is difficult to place Carnegie's ambiguous character in a clearly labeled box. A moralist would, indeed, have a hard time telling whether he was primarily good or evil in any conclusive manner. When one thinks deeply about it, this might apply to just about any of us, albeit on a smaller scale. In the next chapter, let's take a closer look at morality itself, try to understand what its ultimate goals are, and whether it benefits all equally or whether it is typical for a particular social group to benefit from it to the detriment of another.

3

Morality Serves to Coordinate Side-Taking and the Acquisition of Power

Humans have a universal and uniquely nuanced propensity for engaging in social exchanges. The complexity of observed human exchanges requires a brain capable not only of generating and understanding some form of language, but also presents a specific learning capacity for acquiring shared intuitions of justice, or what we call *morality*. For an equitable exchange to take place, one must be able to communicate intentions, be able to evaluate the costs and benefits of things, be able to evaluate others' valuations of the same things, and be able to discern unfairness in the process. Just like the human brain is known to have specific neural networks for speech generation and comprehension, functional imaging and patient studies have led some researchers to conclude that a fairly consistent network of brain regions exists for moral cognition. The proper development of our intuitive moral judgments, just like the proper development of our language ability, requires exposure to a stable social environment during a critical period of early life. In the previous chapter, I mentioned how both abilities can be stunted for life in feral children deprived of normal human interactions in the earlier part of their lives. Our ability for morality, just like our ability for language, has a set of universal features present in all of us, and a range of flexibility to allow for cultural variation. Thus, a baby's brain has skeletal structures capable to discerning and imitating sounds and grammar in human language, and enough flexibility to adopt any language locally spoken within the range of known human languages. In the same way, human children have brain circuitry capable of intuitively grasping moral concepts that are known to be universal, and enough flexibility to also adopt cultural variations of morality. Our intuitive moral judgements are the basis for the development of the complex judicial systems of our modern world.

According to Georgetown University law professor John Mikhail, the intuitive jurisprudence of young children is complex and exhibits many characteristics of a well-developed legal code. For example, three- to four-year-old children use intent or purpose to distinguish two acts that have the same result. They can also distinguish genuine moral violations (such as battery or theft) from violations of social conventions (such as wearing pajamas to school). Four- to five-year-olds use a proportionality principle to determine the correct level of punishment for principals and accessories in a violation. The sense that there is some universality in moral concepts is manifested in the fact that every natural language seems to have words or phrases to express basic deontic concepts, such as *obligatory* (or what one ought to do), *permissible* (or what one may do), and *forbidden* (or what one ought not to do), or their equivalents. Furthermore, prohibitions of murder, rape, and other types of aggression appear to be universal, or nearly so, as are legal distinctions that are based on causation, intention, and voluntary behavior. Both the universality in moral concepts and the presence of intuitive jurisprudence in young children point to innate moral ability in humans.

To make the case that individuals are intuitive lawyers who possess a natural readiness to compute mental representations of human acts in legally cognizable terms, legal scientists present laboratory subjects with what are called *trolley problems*, a well-known family of cases that inquire whether it is permissible to harm one or more individuals in the course of saving others. The moral judgments that these problems elicit are rapid, intuitive, and made with a high degree of certitude. Results indicate that the judgments are widely shared among demographically diverse populations, including young children. Even in large cross-cultural samples, participants' responses to these problems cannot be predicted by variables such as age, sex, gender, race, religion, or education. Furthermore, individuals typically have difficulty producing compelling justifications for these judgments: thus, trolley-problem intuitions exhibit a dissociation between judgments and justifications. To test this for yourself, carefully read each of the problems labeled (a) to (d) and respond *yes* if you think the suggested action is permissible and *no* if not, then compare your answers to the statistics found in research: (a) A runaway trolley is about to run over and kill five people, but the driver can push a button that will turn the trolley into a side track, where it will only kill one person. Is it permissible to push the button? (b) Five patients are dying from organ failure, but a doctor can save all five if she cuts up a sixth healthy person, removes his organs, and distributes them to the other five, killing one but saving five. Is it permissible to do this? (c) A runaway trolley is about to run over and kill five people, but a bystander can throw a switch that will turn the trolley into a side track, where it will kill only one person. Is it permissible to throw the switch? (d) A runaway trolley is about to run over and kill five people, but a bystander who is standing on a footbridge can shove a man in front of the train, saving the five people, but killing the man. Is it permissible to shove the man?

If utilitarian theories of justice—which posit that moral rules are devised to maximize welfare—were correct, one should be answering *yes* to all these questions because the utility of saving five lives is greater than sacrificing one life in all cases presented. Machiavelli would probably have answered that way, as he is known to have said, "It is a sound maxim that reprehensible actions may be justified by their effects, and that when the effect is good . . . it always justifies the action." It turns out that 94 percent of people tested respond *yes* to question (a), 8 percent say *yes* to question (b), 90 percent respond *yes* to question (c), and 10 percent respond the same way to question (d). Most of them cannot explain the difference in their answers when subsequently questioned. In fact, an infinitely large class of such cases can be explained by postulating tacit knowledge of two specific legal rules: the *prohibition of intentional battery* and the *principle of double effect*.

The prohibition of intentional battery forbids purposefully or knowingly causing harmful or offensive contact with another individual or otherwise invading another individual's physical integrity without his or her consent. The principle of double effect is a complex principle of justification, narrower in scope than the traditional necessity defense, which holds that an otherwise prohibited action, such as battery, that has both good and bad effects may be permissible if the prohibited act itself is not directly intended, the good but not the bad effects are directly intended, the good effects outweigh the bad effects, and no morally preferable alternative is available. Cases (b) and (d) represent intentional battery, which we seem to intuitively view as categorically forbidden, no matter the consequences. The *yes* responses to cases (a) and (c) are justified on the basis of the principle of double effect given that the man is killed as a byproduct of an action with good intent, of which the benefit outweighs the cost, and no other alternative is available. Both cases fit a type of scenario which we intuitively seem to view as permissible.

All this implies that moral judgments are not simple, but are intricate and complex and, further, their nuances track dimensions of perpetrators' actions more than welfare outcomes. Notwithstanding these universal dimensions of morality, there is striking cross-cultural variation in moral rules such that behaviors viewed as highly immoral (and punishable) in one group are accepted (even promoted) in other groups, such as the honor killings of women, the extension of interest-bearing loans, or the formation of a militia with the intent to kill homosexuals. Hence, explaining morality in terms of altruism, which is what is usually done, seems inadequate. According to psychology professors Peter DeScioli and Robert Kurzban, altruism theories can potentially explain why people choose actions that benefit other people (as in kinship-based altruism, reciprocal altruism, or competitive altruism), but they do not straightforwardly explain why people show an intense interest in morally judging other people's behavior. Next, altruism theories do not easily explain people's moralistic punishment. Moralistic punishment is puzzling because it is costly for the punisher, given that the punished might seek revenge. Finally, altruism theories do not explain why people often claim that their moral judgments are impartial and independent of their loyalties to the people being judged. Humans try to appear impartial in moral judgments and, at times, they actually show some degree of impartiality, even though they are often partial. Research on hypocrisy shows that people are mostly motivated to appear moral rather than to actually abide by their moral judgments. And research on *motivated reasoning* (a phenomenon consisting in using emotionally biased reasoning to produce justifications or make decisions that are most desired rather than those that accurately reflect the evidence, while still reducing cognitive dissonance) shows that people deviously craft moral justifications to push their own agendas. In short, people can be nice without morality and nasty with morality—kindness and morality are independent. Hence, DeScioli and Kurzban have proposed a theory of moral cognition based on side-taking rather than altruism.

Like many other animal species, humans have disputes over resources, and these conflicts vary in intensity ranging from minor disagreements to heated arguments to lethal violence. Unlike most other animals, humans frequently recruit bystanders for support in disputes, expanding dyadic conflicts to larger ones. This means that individuals must try to reduce not only the costs of their own fights, but also the costs of joining in the fights of others. Choosing sides is a critical decision, because being on the losing side can have high fitness costs, even resulting in death in some cases. When a bystander chooses sides in a conflict, an important consideration is which side other bystanders will support. Bystanders would, indeed, incur greater costs from being on the losing side than the winning side. Numerical superiority would clearly provide an advantage. When all bystanders seek to side with a majority, they collectively face a coordination problem that requires synchronizing their side-taking decisions. They also need to coordinate to avoid the high costs of protracted fights between evenly matched sides. When all bystanders choose the same side, the fight is heavily lopsided and decided quickly with low costs to the bystanders. One strategy that bystanders can use in order to do that is *bandwagoning*, or siding with the more powerful individual based on the relative power of the disputants and their respective supporters. We already learned that humans are built to intuitively rank each other along the power spectrum with a high degree of agreement in power ranking between individuals. When bystanders favor the powerful, however, the strong get stronger as more individuals take their side, creating a feedback loop of increasing power. Use of this decision rule results in a steeply stratified dominance hierarchy, in which the highest-status individual wins all of their disputes, the second-ranked wins against everyone except the first-ranked, and so on until the last-ranked, who always loses. It also creates the problem of despotism: high-status individuals can use their power to monopolize all resources, including food, shelter, and mates. Another approach to choosing sides, which counters despotism, is an *alliance-building strategy*. Here, individuals choose sides based on preexisting alliances and commit to supporting their allies against others when conflicts emerge. Lower-status individuals can, thus, form alliances and commit to side with one another, rather than bandwagon, to defend against despotic individuals. Alliances deflate bullies, but create another problem—when everyone sides with their own family and friends, the group tends to split into evenly matched sides, and fights escalate. This is costly for bystanders because they get scuffed up fighting their friends' battles. *Moral condemnation* offers a third strategy for choosing sides. People can use moral judgment to assess the wrongness of fighters' actions, and then choose sides against whoever was most immoral. When all bystanders use this strategy, they all take the same side and avoid the costs of escalated fighting. That is, moral condemnation functions to synchronize people's side-taking decisions. For moral side-taking to work, the group needs to invent and debate moral rules to cover the most common fights—rules about violence, sex, resources, etc. Thus, the rules consist of a predetermined set of obligatory actions, permissible actions, and forbidden actions for the group. The particular contents of moral rules are not critical to their dynamic coordination function, just as the specific colors of traffic lights are not critical to their function of coordinating driving. *Go* could just as easily be signaled by blue instead of green—all that is required is that the group agrees on the rules. Every new member of the group is informed of the rules from an early age so that they each gain the strength of instinct. Once moral rules are established, people can use accusations of wrongdoing as coercive threats to turn the group—including your family and friends—against you. In sum, moral cognition functions to coordinate condemnation, or synchronized side-taking, not to promote beneficial behavior or to deter harmful behavior, which it sometimes does incidentally. When beneficial or harmless actions provide useful signals for coordinated condemnation, moral cognition will have destructive effects by coordinating aggression toward individuals who have done no harm. Morality has been used to justify anything from gender-based discrimination to hate crimes to terrorism and even genocide. This would make *moral conscience* our evolved strategy to avoid being the victim of such coordinated attacks.

It is a general observation that the moralists often fail to act morally. They are more motivated by seeing others follow their moral rules than following them themselves. When being moral inflicts costs, the practice of *moral hypocrisy*, or masquerading as a moral person while acting immorally, can be advantageous so long as one does not get caught. For a vivid example of moral hypocrisy put into action, let's examine the life of Jean-Jacques Rousseau, the famous philosopher and moral theorist of the Enlightenment. A strong advocate of compassion, pity, equality, justice, and virtue, Rousseau nonetheless persuaded his lover, Thérèse Levasseur, a seamstress, whom he also used as his house servant, to abandon all five of the children she bore him over the years to the Paris Foundling Hospital, an orphanage, immediately upon birth. He convinced Thérèse to do so for the sake of her "honor." Most children abandoned to these institutions in the eighteenth century had a ghastly and short life. Doing this did not stop Rousseau from later publishing a long book about the right way to educate children. Titled *Émile*, it was named after his firstborn son, whom he never got to know. Ironically, his ideas have inspired modern child-centered education. Rousseau is hardly the only person to practice moral hypocrisy. Indeed, research shows that much behavior that has been assumed to be motivated by moral integrity may be motivated by moral hypocrisy instead.

Because novel types of conflicts can arise over time, moral cognition should be capable of generating new moral rules for new dispute types. The openness of moral cognition to new and revised moral rules can give rise to a secondary strategic game, in which individuals seek to establish moral rules that serve their personal interests. The threat of moralistic punishment creates opportunities for those who can influence the set of moral wrongs in their group. By advocating particular moral rules, the weapon of collective punishment can be directed toward behaviors against one's personal interests. This is at the core of the intense competition between powerful individuals in any country today to climb the political ladder. Strong politicians can use their authority and influence to push laws that favor them and their supporters. The veil of impartiality is frequently used to argue that the laws they are pushing benefit everyone equally, when often they do not. Religious leaders of the past have used the very same strategy to push moral rules or values that they and their entourage viewed as favorable. Although they continue to do so today, their influence has been much eroded due to the rise of secularism. In the golden age of religiosity, new prophets appeared almost every day. The "real" ones massacred all the "fake" ones and imposed their interpretation of the universe and their rules on their communities and beyond. Impartiality of the rules was advocated upon the assertion that the rules were directly spoken by a God, who, despite loving every human being equally, had nonetheless specifically chosen them to communicate his words to everyone else.

A 2008 study by Jason Weeden, Adam Cohen, and Douglas Kenrick showed, for instance, that a primary function of religious groups in the contemporary United States is to support low-promiscuity, marriage-centered, heterosexual, high-fertility sexual and reproductive strategies. Religious groups do this through the enforcement of moral norms and the provision of familial support that mitigate the risks and enhance the effectiveness of these strategies. According to the authors, in a sample of 21,131 individuals who participated in the United States General Social Survey, sexual behaviors were the strongest predictor of religious attendance, even after controlling for age and gender. Indeed, effects of age and gender on religious attendance were weaker and substantially reduced when controlling for sexual and family patterns. A sample of 902 college students provided more detailed information on religious, moral, and sexual variables. Results suggested that moral views about sexual behavior were more strongly linked to religious attendance than other moral issues, and mating strategy was more powerful than standard personality variables in predicting religious attendance. Thus, their view is that whatever the evolved sources or historical developments, in the contemporary United States, religious participation has come to serve, among other ends, the goal of buttressing a limited set of competitive sexual and reproductive strategies. Religious institutions try to mitigate risks for those focused on pursuing long-term heterosexual mating strategies through promotion of traditional family morals to limit infidelity—which can mean paternity uncertainty for men and abandonment by a male provider for women—and socioeconomic support to members in need. A central function of the morals promulgated is to impose costs on those pursuing promiscuous, short-term mating strategies. One can do that by advocating for public policies that reduce knowledge of birth control options (by supporting abstinence-only sexual education classes and limiting access to birth control itself), reduce or eliminate abortion services, condemn homosexuality, and generally penalize behaviors closely associated with promiscuous lifestyles among college students—drinking, drug usage, cursing, and lying to and disobeying parents. Coordinated condemnation of short-term mating strategies, thus, appears to be a central feature of today's religious morals in the United States.

Organized religion, which has held supreme power over popular morality for the past two millennia, owes its spectacular success, at least in part, to the promulgation of the interests of large groups of people throughout the world. Historically, and even today, the largest such group has been the one comprising the world's poor. Friedrich Nietzsche took the position that religious morality was the instrument through which the world's weak and oppressed banded together against the strong and fortunate in their quest for power. To that end he asks, "Whose will to power does morality represent?" And to which he responds, "The answer is that three corresponding powers lie behind it: (1) the instinctive opposition of the herd to the strong, independent men; (2) the instinctive opposition of the suffering and unfortunate to the fortunate; (3) the instinctive opposition of the mediocre to the exceptional.

46

. . . By what means does a virtue come into power? By precisely the same means as a political party: through defamation, suspicion, undermining those virtues already in power which strive against it, rechristening them with new names, systemic persecution and ridicule, thence by flagrant immorality." Machiavelli concurs when he says, "The old religion did not beatify men unless they were replete with worldly glory: army commanders, for instance, and rulers of republics. Our religion has glorified humble and contemplative men, rather than men of action. It has assigned as man's highest good humility, abnegation, and contempt for mundane things, whereas the other identified it with magnanimity, bodily strength, and everything else that conduces to make men bold." Nietzsche's assumption that the world's strong were simply duped and became weak themselves by espousing the virtues of the weak, is, however, dubious. Strength means primarily intellectual strength among humans. It is, therefore, difficult to imagine that the intellectually superior should be so easily duped by their inferiors. Instead, it is more likely that the powerful classes themselves saw an opportunity in religion to hang on to power. Machiavelli understood this better than anyone else: "This pattern of life, therefore, appears to have made the world weak and to have handed it over as a pray to the wicked, who run it successfully and seamlessly since they are well aware that the generality of men, with paradise for their goal, consider how best to bear, rather than how best to avenge, their injuries." The rulers of ancient Rome clearly understood that it was easier to police religious masses than masses of nonbelievers. Thus, Machiavelli states: "It will also be seen by those who pay attention to Roman history how much religion helped in the control of armies, in encouraging the plebs, in producing good men, and in shaming the bad." Fast-forward a few centuries, Karl Marx seems to be oddly echoing Machiavelli when he states that "Religion . . . is the opiate of the masses." Marx believed that religion had certain practical functions in society that were similar to the function of opium in a sick or injured person—it reduced people's immediate suffering and provided them with pleasant illusions, which gave them the strength to carry on. Marx also saw religion as harmful to his revolutionary goals, as it prevented people from seeing the class structure and oppression around them, thus hampering the socialist revolution. With the rise of Marxism at the beginning of the twentieth century, it was then finally that the oppressed saw religion as a tool of their oppressors. How could organized religion not be eminently successful when it promoted the interests of so many human groups across the millennia, from the highest social classes to the lowest and many more people with seemingly opposing stakes?

Morality has preceded the establishment of today's formal laws and justice systems. It has always been a central theme of religious movements, which are the precedents of today's formal political movements. Otherwise stated, morality and religion are the antiquated versions of modern power structures—the legal system and the political system, respectively. Most religions will have lists for their followers to internalize—lists of sins or vices and of preferred values or virtues. Vices are generally meant to represent prohibited, antisocial behaviors, while virtues represent prosocial behaviors, meaning ones that are beneficial to the group and which one ought to display. Another way to define vices is to recognize that they represent those behaviors that the group considers to be immoral or evil, making virtues the set of moral or good behaviors preferred by the group. But we now know that morality has both universal elements, which tend to benefit all members of a group more or less equally, and group-specific or cultural elements, which tend to primarily benefit a subset of group members to the detriment of others. When morality frequently put the interests of a specific, power-hungry group ahead of yours and of those who resemble you, immorality may simply be a sign of discernment and, ultimately, intelligence—a victory of independent thought over an internalized sense of duty to an oppressor. Good and evil are never absolutes. They represent relative constructs, always imbued with cultural flavors, and meant to facilitate group consensus in conflict resolution. When evolutionary fitness is at stake and morality determines who comes out ahead, determining the moral code in one's community becomes a power game. Whilst all of us seek power in some way, including via manipulation of moral rules, are some of us more attuned to power relationships than others? Do we all aspire to high status with the same fervor? Or are some of us biologically more inclined and capable to do the hard work needed to attain the highest-possible level of power? Let's explore these questions next.

II

Power Seekers Are Different: The Biological Basis of Dominance Motivation

4

Cognitive Empathy

Although power is desirable to all, some people do seem to seek it more intently and fervently than others. From an early age, they display extreme self-confidence, social aloofness, competitiveness, a craving for fame and admiration, and a burning desire for status, wealth, influence, control, and ultimately power. They differ from the rest of the population by the lengths they are willing to go in order to obtain power. These individuals, who are endowed with an extreme temperamental variant, if blessed with other qualities such as high intelligence, creativity, or talent, and presented with the right opportunities, can become the rich and famous geniuses in the arts, science, sports, business, and politics. According to psychiatrist Nicholas Pediaditakis, persons with a similar temperament but who lack additional qualities or opportunities, form a common pool of individuals who are at increased risk for a major mental disorder. This squarely puts the perceived success or failure at gaining power—probably modulated by the hard-charging individual's resiliency, or stress tolerance—at the very heart of many mental disorders. If we are innately attuned to signs of status in ourselves and others from a very early age, it should not be surprising that this might be the case.

Temperament is defined as the particular inborn behavioral propensities for each individual, which act as an unfinished scaffold upon which the *character* of the person is formed over the course of life. Along with the remaining genetics of the individual, it guides the environmental influences, including learned attitudes and moral codes that are ultimately embedded into the scaffold to form the final personality in adulthood. Research shows that 50 percent of our personality traits are, indeed, determined genetically, the remaining 50 percent being forged by random and unsystematic environmental influences. Temperament is made of two distinct clusters of traits, which each originate from separate evolutionary pressures. The first cluster originates from evolutionary pressures for self-preservation, selfishness, aloofness, and perhaps even aggressiveness towards others. The second cluster emanates from the evolutionary pressure to be an accepted member of a social group and includes such traits as sociability, connectedness, cooperation, empathy, and altruism. Given the ever-changing nature of environmental conditions, the long-run survival of an ancestral tribe crucially depended on variability of the temperamental traits between its members, irrespective of advantage or disadvantage to the individuals themselves. This flexibility is achieved when each trait is allowed to exist on a continuum, sometimes, resulting in lopsided temperamental types—for instance, introverts versus extroverts.

Creative geniuses and individuals at risk for major mental disorders have an extreme variant of the inborn temperament. This extreme variant lies beyond the normally occurring temperamental variability. These individuals are, to various degrees, less social, more self-centered, and aloof. They are generally deficient in empathy, although they may exhibit remarkable learned affability and civility. They tend to think the world, rather than feel it. When they do feel the world, they often do so inappropriately, in disproportion to what their circumstances would normally warrant. Schizophrenia (characterized by flat affect and extreme distrust of others to the point of paranoia); bipolar disorder (marked by alternating episodes of abnormally elevated mood and activity, or *mania*, and abnormally low mood and activity, or *depression*); obsessive-compulsive disorder (in which a person experiences repeated, intrusive thoughts or sensations, called *obsessions*, and the urge to perform certain routines repeatedly, called *compulsions*, usually, as a way of coping with the obsessions); and the dark triad consisting of narcissism (characterized by entitlement, superiority, and dominance); Machiavellianism (marked by glib social charm and manipulativeness); and psychopathy (known for callous social attitudes, impulsivity, and interpersonal antagonism) are conditions that develop most frequently in the vulnerable individuals. These conditions can overlap or switch from one to another and are known to have a common neurodevelopmental origin. Additionally, individuals presenting with autism spectrum disorders are also known to be deficient in empathy. Those diagnosed with high-functioning autism, when also endowed with high intelligence, can muster extreme attention to detail, focus, and pattern-finding abilities, which can turn them into celebrities in their complex professional fields. Elon Musk, the billionaire serial entrepreneur, and Bill Gross, the world-famous bond manager, are two such celebrities who have discussed their diagnoses as high-functioning autistic individuals and have credited their emphatic deficiencies (along with other traits) with contributing to their enormous success.

A large portion of our brain's function is normally allocated for social intercourse, meaning the give-and-take exchanges involved in all social relationships. The absence or deficiency of the social algorithms in brain function frees enormous power in the brain of these temperamentally lop-sided individuals, which then becomes available for creative or competitive goals. Unencumbered by the care of others, they instead have abundant time to focus on self-development, competition, creativity, and problem-solving. Their obsessional tendencies—which can make them prone to developing harmful addictions—directed toward solving a particular problem or achieving a specific goal is the very source of their seemingly unbreakable motivation and ruthless persistence in the face of adversity. When deficient in normal fear response, or abnormally impulsive, they can take risks that a more neurotypical person would refrain from. Although this can result in great harm to oneself or others on most occasions, it can pay enormous dividends in rare instances. Having few qualms about the feelings of others gives them large latitude to engage in exploitative social strategies to get what they want. False emotions associated with empathy can be displayed without the individuals actually feeling an emotional response. This can be beneficial in social situations where certain emotional responses are expected. As these individuals often display a tendency for social dominance, their emphatic deficiencies can also make it easier for them to control and manipulate social resources within the hierarchy through the use of a mix of prosocial and coercive social strategies, which is technically referred to as being a *bi-strategic controller*. When also endowed with exuberant confidence, guile, and charm, such individuals can sometimes turn into charismatic national leaders or religious figures. Examples include Alexander the Great, Abraham Lincoln, and Theodore Roosevelt, all of whom are known to have had mood disorders, sometimes, with psychotic features. With extraordinary visuospatial abilities and schizoid tendencies (a mild precursor to schizophrenia), they can become renowned scientists. Isaac Newton, Charles Darwin, and Nikola Tesla all fit the bill. Those with artistic talent and cyclothymic tendencies (a mild precursor of bipolar disorder) may turn into celebrated poets or painters or musicians. Lord Byron, Virginia Woolf, Vincent van Gogh, and Beethoven are prominent examples, all known to experience bipolar episodes. A deeper look into the lives of any of the robber barons—the wealthy and powerful American businessmen of the late nineteenth and early twentieth centuries—will reveal strong dark triad tendencies. Examples include Andrew Carnegie, John D. Rockefeller, J. P. Morgan, Cornelius Vanderbilt, and Henry Ford.

Dysfunctional emotion regulation is the common denominator of the aforementioned mental disorders. This dysfunction may manifest itself as a deficiency in recognizing, describing, and attending to one's own emotions, which is called *alexithymia*, or as a deficiency in empathy, meaning the inability or limited ability to feel and understand the emotions of another. Empathy has two distinct components: *affective empathy*, involving the capacity to experience the emotions of another, and *cognitive empathy*, encompassing the understanding of others' emotional states. It is in affective empathy that most of these individuals seem deficient. Although these traits appear to be maladaptive when considered within the psychiatric realm, they may actually be quite adaptive if coupled with certain other traits and considered within certain environmental conditions. Indeed, they may verily provide a competitive advantage by facilitating behavior associated with the attainment of goals that require exploitation of others and with the pursuit of a short-term mating strategy. They are only maladaptive when bestowed upon the wrong individuals—those whose remaining traits make them unfit for the fast, turbulent, competitive, ever-changing, and, in a way, stressful life strategy—or when the affected individual is constrained to exist in the wrong environment. Their most extreme manifestations may also make them maladaptive, while moderately high versions can confer an advantage. For instance, while mania is a severe psychiatric condition, its milder version, *hypomania*, can confer tremendous advantage both socially and professionally thanks to the elevated energy, mood, drive, sociability, self-confidence, and focus that come with it. Hypomania may actually be a core component of falling in love and may have originally been evolved to facilitate reproduction.

Empathy is central to social interactions. In 2009, Simone Shamay-Tsoory from the University of Haifa in Israel and collaborators published the results of an experiment, which showed that affective and cognitive empathy are processed by two separate brain regions that function independently: an early emotional contagion system to support our ability to empathize emotionally, or feel what others feel, and a more advanced cognitive perspective-taking system to understand what others feel. In humans, just as in other species, imitation constitutes a core learning process and involves special brain cells called *mirror neurons*. Here is how imitation is presumed to occur: perception of a behavior in another automatically activates one's own mental representations for the behavior, and output from this shared representation automatically proceeds to motor areas of the brain where responses are prepared and executed. This state-matching reaction proceeds through the mirror neurons of the brain located in an area of the human prefrontal cortex—our brain's executive and control center—called the *inferior frontal gyrus* (IFG). The mirror neurons in the IFG are also activated when we recognize an emotion in another and automatically trigger the same emotion in us, which is known as *emotional contagion*. It is by, literally, feeling what the other person feels that we become aware of their emotional state. This is the basis of affective empathy.

It gives us an emotional stake in the other person's circumstances and, perhaps, makes us want to come to their help. It makes us care about other people's distress. The human empathic response is, however, more than pure emotional contagion and involves cognitive perspective-taking (which is sometimes called *theory of mind*). Cognitive perspective-taking is the ability to understand that others have mental states—meaning emotions, beliefs, thoughts, and desires—that are, sometimes, different from our own. When coupled with affective empathy, it helps in, first, understanding that what we feel as a result of emotional contagion is not due to our own circumstances, but to those of the other person. This is what allows us to place ourselves in the other person's shoes and understand why they feel the way they do given their circumstances. We can then infer the intensions of the other person by imagining what actions they are likely to take in the future based on their current mental state. Cognitive empathy alone is a colder, more detached way of relating to others. People who are proficient in cognitive empathy, but deficient in affective empathy, will not feel what a neighbor in distress may feel. As a result, they will remain cold-blooded while witnessing the neighbor's suffering. They can, however, understand the facts of the neighbor's circumstances, retrieve from memory how they may have themselves reacted in similar past circumstances via pattern matching, and predict how the neighbor may react as a result of their contingencies. The brain area called the *ventromedial prefrontal cortex* (VM) has been shown to be activated when we engage in cognitive empathy. Whereas emotional contagion, the lowest common denominator of all empathic responses, is reported in such primitive species as birds and rodents, perspective-taking abilities are evident only in more phylogenetically advanced mammals, such as the great apes. Accordingly, human babies show emotional contagion in response to the distress of another individual without being able to separate their own and the other's distress. Only later, during childhood and adolescence, do individuals become increasingly more capable of taking the other individual's perspective. In their experiment, Shamay-Tsoory and her collaborators assessed subjects with localized damage limited to either the VM or IFG cortices and two control groups (one without any brain damage and the other with lesions in a brain area not involved in empathy) with measures of empathy that incorporated both cognitive and affective dimensions. Patients with VM damage showed consistent and selective deficit in cognitive empathy and theory of mind, while presenting with intact emotion recognition and affective empathy. Patients with IFG lesions, on the other hand, displayed extremely impaired affective empathy and emotion recognition and no impairment in cognitive empathy. Their study is important because it confirmed the fact that affective and cognitive empathy are not just theoretical constructs, but biological ones subserved by two separate cortical areas. Equally important was their discovery that these two areas function independently from one another, as damage to one does not impair the ability of the other to perform its function. This is the biological basis for the observed fact that one can be proficient in one type of empathy and deficient in the other.

In an effort to clarify the emotional deficiencies related to limited empathy and alexithymia in individuals presenting dark triad traits associated with narcissism, Machiavellianism, and psychopathy, researchers Peter Jonason and Laura Krause conducted a correlational study of 320 volunteers to an online survey. Alexithymia is thought to have three parts: difficulty identifying one's own feelings, difficulty describing one's feelings, and externally oriented thinking. The researchers surmised these three traits to be positively correlated with the dark triad. Arguably, the capacity to identify or understand one's own emotions (i.e., alexithymia) may be linked to the capacity to identify or understand others' feelings (i.e., empathy); that is, the ability to put oneself in someone else's shoes may be underpinned by the ability to first have knowledge of one's own shoes. In addition, an externally focused thinking style may reduce the capacity to recognize and attend to both one's own and others' emotional states, thus impacting empathy. The study revealed that each dark triad trait was associated with a unique pattern of emotional deficits. Psychopathy was correlated with limited overall empathy (both affective and cognitive), difficulty describing feelings, and externally oriented thinking. Narcissism was associated with limited affective empathy and difficulty identifying feelings, whereas

Machiavellianism was associated with externally oriented thinking. Jonason and Krause contend that the links between the dark triad traits and emotional deficiencies are indicative of an adaptive role for the traits. That is, having low levels of empathy and a limited ability or motivation to communicate one's emotions to others facilitates the antagonistic social strategy embodied in the dark triad traits. Indeed, the external orientation they utilize may indicate that those high on the dark triad—psychopaths in particular—spend little time considering their internal world and instead are more focused on getting what they want from the external world. In other words, too much time spent being concerned about the feelings of oneself or others may be an obstacle for someone pursuing the fast-life strategy embodied by the dark triad. Compared to women, men score consistently higher on dark triad traits and alexithymia and lower on empathy. Both sexes utilize selfish and exploitative goal-directed strategies, but differential evolutionary needs may have created disparate correlations and underlying mechanisms behind these strategies, with varying levels of emotional connectedness being required for men and women to achieve their goals. Their study revealed that the dark triad manifests itself primarily in the form of narcissism in women and psychopathy in men. Theoretically, this could be linked to the differing evolutionary pressures presented to and, thus, divergent adaptive strategies developed by each sex. Historically, men's needs were met through a "hunter" approach, whereby they directly attained material goods from the external world, and sociality was useful, but not essential, whereas women's needs may have been more effectively met through social belongingness, serving to protect and provide for both themselves and their offspring parasitically through others. Therefore, the profound lack of empathy associated with psychopathy could be adaptive for achievement of overtly exploitative "male" goals, with relatively higher levels of empathy and narcissism better suited to meet the covertly exploitative "female" goals.

The traits associated with the dark triad of narcissism, Machiavellianism, and psychopathy are of particular interest in the context of seeking power, as those pursuing power most avidly or successfully seem to display them to varying degrees. In fact, the behavior pattern of the hard-charging type-A person—extremes of aggressiveness, easily aroused hostility, a sense of time urgency, and competitive striving for achievement—presents remarkable overlap with the behavior pattern associated with Machiavellianism. Both include aspects of dominance, both emphasize competitiveness, striving for achievement, and a sense of personal control over the events of life. In 1985, Douglas Madsen, professor of political science at the University of Iowa, wanted to find out whether individuals with the type-A personality were biologically different from the rest of the population. Experiments previously done at the University of California in Los Angeles on male vervet monkeys had shown that, among captive male vervets, there is a clear biochemical marker for dominance, namely the level of serotonin in the blood, referred to as *whole blood serotonin* (WBS). Serotonin is a biochemical agent having neuroregulatory functions in both humans and other animals. It is found in the central nervous system, in the blood, and in several other locations in the body. Its biological function is complex and multifaceted, modulating mood, cognition, reward, learning, memory, and numerous physiological processes, such as vomiting and vasoconstriction. In male vervet monkeys, elevated serotonin in the blood was correlated with a repertoire of behaviors closely tied to dominance, such as approaching others, not avoiding others who come near, and initiating aggression. Most interestingly, serotonin levels tracked changes in status: dominant males who became nondominant exhibited a decline in WBS, whereas nondominant animals who became dominant showed the reverse. This finding motivated Madsen to find out whether whole blood serotonin was also a marker of type-A personality in humans. His experiment took place at a hospital. He recruited seventy-two male undergraduate students whom he graded on type-A traits via a questionnaire. The students were broken into twelve groups of six men. Each group was processed on a separate day, but at the same time of the day. Each was directed to devise group solutions to very difficult logic puzzles. For each puzzle, only ten minutes were allowed. For a puzzle solution to be registered by a group, at least five of the six members had to vote in favor of that solution. Thereafter, one person in the group had to report the group's solution and why it was the only correct one. Each group was videotaped to assess the relationship between psychological stress levels and distributions of influence within the group. A sample of blood was also taken from each subject every twenty minutes throughout the session. The results showed strong correlations between high WBS levels and high scores on type-A traits. Madsen's experiment revealed a striking portrait of the kind of person one would intuitively take to be power-oriented. Hard-charging, competitive, impatient, aggressive, distrustful of others, and confident—all in all a remarkable mix and one readily tied to Machiavellianism, lacking only evidence of the ruthless and manipulative aspects to make the match very close. More importantly, the findings were the first systematic evidence of any biochemical property in humans which differentiates power seekers from others, namely high levels of whole blood serotonin.

In summary, power seekers truly are different. Their hard-charging style has biological and evolutionary underpinnings. They present emotional deficiencies, which are adaptive for their fast-life strategy. They tend to pay little attention to their own feelings or to other people's feelings. Having externally oriented thinking and limited affective empathy, they are generally unconcerned with the care of others, preferring to relate to them in a colder, more detached way instead via cognitive empathy. Unencumbered by the care of others, they have full freedom to devote themselves entirely to the pursuit of power, which may put them in especially stressful situations more often than the rest of the population. Given that they appear also to be endowed with eccentric traits characteristic of a number of mental illnesses, their tendency to avidly pursue power may, sometimes, come at substantial personal costs. If power seekers differ from everybody else in the way that they relate to others, do they also differ from them in the way that they deal with challenge or adversity? Let's explore this topic in the next chapter.

5

Grit and Resilience

As hard-charging, competitive, aggressive, and confident as those avidly seeking power may be, some ultimately end up being more successful in gaining power than others. This begs the question of what differentiates the ultimate winners from the losers. Intelligence, as measured by the intelligence quotient (IQ), is the best documented predictor of achievement, accounting for up to one-third of the variance in some measures of success. IQ is found to be strongly correlated with a wide range of achievement outcomes, including college and graduate school grade point average, income, career potential, job performance, and choice of occupation. The predictive validities of intelligence are found to rise with the complexity of the occupation considered. In addition to cognitive ability, a list of attributes of high-achieving individuals would likely include creativity, vigor, emotional intelligence, charisma, self-confidence, emotional stability, physical attractiveness, and other positive qualities. Besides individual characteristics, a number of situational factors and social and cultural variables—such as country of birth, parental socioeconomic status, or social connectedness—can also account for the variance in degrees of achievement. On an individual level, some traits seem more crucial than others for particular vocations. Extraversion may be fundamental to a career in sales, for instance, but irrelevant to a career in creative writing. However, some traits might be essential to success no matter the domain. In a paper published in 2007, Angela Duckworth and collaborators suggested that one personal quality is shared by the most prominent leaders in every field: grit. The researchers defined *success* and *achievement* to refer to the accomplishment of widely valued goals and *grit* as perseverance and passion for long-term goals.

Grit entails working strenuously toward challenges, maintaining effort and interest over years despite failure, adversity, and plateaus in progress. The gritty individual approaches achievement as a marathon; his or her advantage is stamina. Whereas disappointment or boredom signals to others that it is time to change trajectory and cut losses, the gritty individual stays the course. When Duckworth interviewed professionals in investment banking, painting, journalism, academia, medicine, and law, grit or a close synonym was cited as often as talent when asked about what quality distinguished star performers in their respective fields. In fact, many noted with surprise that prodigiously gifted peers did not end up in the upper echelons of their field. In fields such as business, where an average IQ is more than enough to satisfy the cognitive requirements, disparity in grit may well be the difference between success and mediocrity. The concept of grit has some overlap with the personality trait of *conscientiousness*. Conscientious individuals are characteristically thorough, careful, reliable, organized, industrious, and self-controlled. Grit overlaps with the achievement aspects of conscientiousness, but differs in its emphasis on long-term stamina, rather than short-term intensity. The study by Duckworth and collaborators revealed that grit accounted for an average of 4 percent of the variance in success outcomes (including educational attainment) among two large samples of adults, grade point average among Ivy League undergraduates, retention in two classes of cadets at West Point, and ranking in the National Spelling Bee. Within intensely competitive environments, such as in American college football, a 4 percent variance among players may well mean the difference between making the cut for the National Football League or not. The researchers reached the reasonable conclusion that the achievement of difficult goals entails not only talent, but also the sustained and focused application of talent over time.

The advice to persevere despite adversity should, however, come with a couple caveats. Firstly, one ought to choose wisely where to put forth effort. Repetitive jobs with little training requirements are hardly conducive to fame and fortune. Secondly, achieving excellence in a job at which few are successful requires that one has a natural ability to do it with far more ease than the average person. What each of us is capable of doing today depends greatly upon what the people that preceded us did. If the requirements of the job are well above our genetic propensities, persevering despite constant struggle and repeated failure is nonsensical self-mutilation. Given that we can only become aware of our abilities through trial and error, it behooves us to acquire a sense of when it may be best to cut our losses and move on to something else. This is where a hard-charging young person may struggle and, sometimes, get hurt in the course of trying to accrue power.

The concept of grit is related to the much more researched concept of *resilience*, which comes into play when one is confronted with elevated stress or adversity. After all, it is difficult to maintain stamina if one breaks down mentally in the face of the smallest adversity one encounters. While some individuals develop psychiatric conditions, such as post-traumatic stress disorder (PTSD) or major depressive disorder (MDD), others recover from stressful experiences without displaying significant symptoms of psychological ailments, demonstrating stress resilience. *Resilience* is defined as successful adaptation or the absence of a pathological outcome following exposure to stressful or potentially traumatic life events or life circumstances. Thus, it involves both the capacity to maintain a healthy outcome following exposure to adversity and the capacity to rebound after a negative experience. This brings forth the question of whether resilience is purely inborn and inherited or whether it can be fostered through experience. In other words, why are some individuals more resilient than others?

In a multiyear longitudinal study of a national sample, Mark Seery and collaborators found that people with a history of *some* lifetime adversity reported better mental health and well-being outcomes than not only people with a high history of adversity, but also people with no history of adversity. These results can be explained in terms of developing psychological tough-ness with early exposure to moderate stressors. Exposure to stressors has a positive toughening effect when the exposure is limited, with an opportunity for recovery. Toughness leaves individuals more likely to appraise situations positively, more emotionally stable, and better able to cope psychologically and physiologically with difficult stressors and minor challenges, relative to unhardened individuals. It seems that what does not kill us may truly make us stronger. Both sheltering from all stressors during childhood and continuous exposure to stressors leads to lack of toughness. Sheltering provides no opportunity to develop mastery over adversity and is unlikely to persist indefinitely, so when stressors are eventually encountered, individuals are likely to be ill-equipped to cope with them. In that sense, the development of psychological toughness is analogous to the development of physical fitness from aerobic exercise: excessive exercise exerts a harmful toll on the body, but fitness does not improve with inactivity. The researchers surmise that experiencing low, but nonzero, levels of adversity could teach effective coping skills, help engage social support networks, create a sense of mastery over past adversity, foster beliefs in the ability to cope successfully in the future, and, thus, generate psychophysiological toughness. All of these qualities should contribute to resilience in the face of subsequent major adversity. Such qualities should also make subsequent minor daily hassles seem more manageable, rather than overwhelming, leading to benefits for overall mental health and well-being. At the biological level, toughening could proceed through the process of epigenetics, where environmental influences can permanently change the expression of certain portions of DNA. Some of these changes in gene expression can become inheritable, leading to genetically toughened offspring. Having said that, how low or high should the early stressors be in order to foster toughness, rather than bring about illness? While some military personnel seem capable of resilience in the face of what would be considered extremely traumatic experiences by most people, some seem to break down in relatively minor combat situations. In the same vein, many children seem to grow into resilient and successful adults despite an extremely challenging childhood. In fact, both Andrew Carnegie and Jean-Jacques Rousseau, both of whom I mentioned earlier among other successful individuals, have had to fend for themselves starting from their early teens. Given that 50 percent of our psychological traits are genetically determined, it is likely that each of us is endowed with a genetically set stress threshold, beyond which we become susceptible to developing psychiatric conditions. The degree to which resilience can be fostered through life experience should, therefore, vary with individual genetics. Indeed, resilience has been shown to have substantial inborn or biological correlations.

The human stress response—also called the fight-or-flight response—is an evolved physiological response to help us deal with situations of stress. When we face a threatening or stressful event, the hypothalamus, a small gland within the brain's limbic system (located under the cortex), releases a peptide hormone and neurotransmitter known as the corticotropin-releasing hormone (CRH). The CRH is transported into the pituitary gland, an endocrine gland located just under the hypothalamus, where it stimulates the production of another hormone known as adrenocorticotropic hormone (ACTH). The ACTH then makes its way from the brain to the adrenal glands—two triangular-shaped endocrine glands situated just above our kidneys—via the bloodstream, where it stimulates production of two steroid hormones, cortisol and dehydroepiandrosterone (DHEA), and two catecholamines, called norepinephrine and epinephrine, all of which play important roles in the stress response. Norepinephrine is particularly noted for its function in cognitive alertness and vigilant concentration in individuals under stress. It modulates the fight-or-flight response along with epinephrine by immediately increasing the heart rate, pressing the liberation of glucose from energy stores to power the response, and increasing blood and oxygen supply to the muscles and the brain. Higher activation of the norepinephrine system in the brain is known for inhibiting functions in the prefrontal cortex and, therefore, promoting faster, instinctual responses over more complex and slower cognitive responses. Cortisol's primary function is to mobilize and replenish energy stores. Cortisol is also known to perform an important role in the stress response by way of significant increases in vigilance, increased arousal, consolidation of memory, and selective attention. DHEA helps in the control of fatness, mineral metabolism, sexual functioning, and has effects similar to anti-inflammatories and antioxidants. According to a 2016 review paper by Carlos Osorio and collaborators, DHEA may also exert a protective response against stress. Research supports the view that resilient individuals have superior endocrine regulation in response to stressful situations compared to less-resilient persons.

Resilience involves a faster and more robust increase in levels of cortisol, epinephrine, and norepinephrine in response to CRH and ACTH release by the brain. It also involves a more efficient return back to the baseline for these hormones once the threat is overcome. If recovery is not accompanied by an adequate homeostatic response, which is mediated by DHEA, the initial response could ultimately result in harmful aftereffects. Repeated chronic exposure to heightened neuroendocrine responses to stress can result in psychopathological conditions such as PTSD and MDD, in addition to diseases such as high blood pressure, diabetes, and heart conditions. Clinical evidence suggests that abnormal regulation of brain norepinephrine systems is observed in patients with PTSD, manifested through symptoms such as frightening flashbacks, heightened arousal, elevated heart rate, increased blood pressure, and excessive sweating. Prolonged exposure to high levels of cortisol is known to have significant toxic effects, causing neuronal degeneration in the hippocampus—a brain area involved in memory and learning—resulting in memory and learning deficits. Abnormally high levels of cortisol along with cognitive deficits, such as problems with memory and concentration, have been observed in patients with depression. Research findings indicate that adrenal DHEA plays a crucial role in modulating the negative effects of cortisol and is associated with resilience. Studies conducted on healthy military personnel undergoing stressful training and evaluations revealed that soldiers who performed better under acute stress had higher levels of DHEA or a higher DHEA-to-cortisol ratio in the blood. Other studies have reported that a reduced DHEA-to-cortisol ratio can be translated into a higher risk of experiencing chronic fatigue syndrome, anxiety, anorexia nervosa, depression, schizophrenia, and PTSD. It appears that resilient individuals may have adrenal glands capable of ensuring a better balance between cortisol and DHEA in stressful situations.

In addition to DHEA, two neurotransmitters, known as neuropeptide-Y and galanin, are also believed to be associated with resilience. Neuropeptide-Y is thought to have several important functions, including reducing anxiety, stress, pain perception, circadian rhythms, and blood pressure. According to Osorio and collaborators, numerous studies have proven the valuable function of neuropeptide-Y in mediating resilience and vulnerability to stress in both animals and humans. For instance, studies were conducted on military personnel participating in a particularly stressful training, known as Survival, Evasion, Resistance, and Escape (SERE), to compare highly resilient members of the United States Special Forces with their regular infantry counterparts. The Special Forces participants were shown to produce higher concentrations of neuropeptide-Y and exhibit an enhanced physical and psychological performance, followed by a reduced vulnerability to stress-induced anxiety and dissociation. In addition, the neuropeptide galanin also appears to have a protective effect during the stress response. It is released in the brain when the locus coeruleus, a brain area believed to be involved in both panic attacks and the stress response, releases high levels of norepinephrine. Consequently, its activity reduces the firing action of the locus coeruleus, thereby modulating behaviors resembling anxiety. In summary, particularly resilient individuals may have brains capable of establishing superior balance between the anxiety-inducing agent norepinephrine and anxiety-reducing ones, such as neuropeptide-Y and galanin, in response to stressful situations.

Finally, resilient individuals may be endowed with brains capable of the improved regulation of two other neurotransmitters, serotonin and dopamine, which are heavily involved in numerous mental illnesses, such as bipolar disorder, depression, schizophrenia, anxiety disorders, and PTSD, as well as the general stress response. Dopamine is implicated in various neural functions, including attention, motivation, and motor control. Stress inhibits the release of dopamine in the nucleus accumbens, an area mainly associated with the reward pathway, and activates the release of dopamine in the medial prefrontal cortex, an area associated with complex cognitive behavior, personality expression, decision-making, and moderating social behavior. According to Osorio and collaborators, significantly reduced prefrontal dopamine levels lead to the maintenance of the fear response, an outcome normally observed in individuals with PTSD. Conversely, studies that identified abnormally high levels of dopamine release in the medial prefrontal cortex resulted in cognitive impairment, an outcome observed in individuals suffering from schizophrenia. Thus, the data suggest that there is an optimal range for stress-induced increases in dopamine released in the medial prefrontal cortex that may facilitate advantageous behavioral responses in resilient individuals. As for serotonin, it is known to have an effect on the regulation of appetite, sleep, and feelings of well-being and happiness. It is also known for its effects on mood and anxiety. The acute stress response is linked with augmented serotonin turnover in different areas of the brain, particularly in the lateral hypothalamus, amygdala (which control the fear response and other emotions), nucleus accumbens, and the prefrontal cortex. The liberation of serotonin in the brain is known to have both anxiety-inducing and anxiety-reducing effects, and this outcome is mediated by which part of the forebrain and receptors are stimulated. It appears that a resilient brain is one that can skillfully manage stimulation of serotonin receptors in the forebrain during the stress response.

Let's now recall the 1985 experiment by Douglas Madsen of the University of Iowa (from the last chapter), in which he demonstrated that power seeking, meaning the pursuit of social dominance, has a biochemical marker, namely whole blood serotonin (WBS). Madsen also measured blood levels of ACTH, norepinephrine, epinephrine, and cortisol in his subjects during the stressful sessions, where they solved difficult logic problems in groups of six. In a subsequent paper that he published in 1986, his results showed that those scoring high on type-A traits, in addition to having high WBS, exhibited special physiological activation in the face of challenge. Their blood concentration of both ACTH and cortisol rapidly rose well above the levels observed in the rest of the subjects during the challenge and were brought back just as rapidly to a prechallenge baseline afterwards, which is possibly indicative of a superior regulation of their stress response compared to other study participants. A well-managed stress response may be especially important to successfully pursuing social dominance strategies, as power seekers tend to be above average risk-takers and are, thus, likely to frequently find themselves in high-stress situations. The quality of their endocrine system may well be the difference between winners and losers among those motivated by social dominance, as the quest for power, sometimes, comes with the steep price of developing mental illness. Let's further explore the risk appetites of these hard-charging individuals in the next chapter.

6

Risk-Taking

An individual's *propensity to take risks* is the degree to which the individual is willing to expose himself or herself to the possibility of loss, injury, or other adverse or unwelcome circumstance for the chance of realizing a gain or otherwise improving his or her circumstances. Reckless risks are those that involve a high degree of loss for a chance at minimal gain. They represent the kind of actions that an impulsive and, perhaps, unintelligent or careless individual may engage in. When it is worth taking, risk is positively correlated with reward, meaning the greater the risk, the greater the potential for loss, and the greater the reward or gain. Risky enterprises have a high degree of uncertainty embedded in them and usually present a small chance of a very positive outcome and a much bigger chance of failure, sometimes resulting in large losses. Most people are risk-avoidant, meaning they will generally prefer to engage in actions that have more certain outcomes, despite the fact that they also result in lower payoffs. Particularly powerful individuals tend to have a lopsided share of resources and influence compared to their low-power peers, indicating a significantly higher propensity to take risks—at least, when the power has been acquired through their own efforts and not simply inherited or gained by mere chance. The behavior pattern of the power-seeking type-A person—extremes of aggressiveness, easily aroused hostility, a sense of time urgency, and competitive striving for achievement—would also suggest a natural willingness to take greater risks for the possibility of achieving fame and fortune. Research indicates that the propensity for aggressiveness and risk-taking may have a significant genetic basis.

Monoamine oxidase A, also known as MAO-A, is an *enzyme* that in humans is coded by the MAOA *gene*. MAO-A (the enzyme) is a key regulator for normal brain function, as it degrades neurotransmitters such as dopamine, norepinephrine, and serotonin, which are known to play key roles in the regulation of mood, emotions, arousal, and motivation. Too little enzyme means too many of these neurotransmitters in the brain, while too much enzyme means overly aggressive degradation—hence, too few neurotransmitters. Both spell trouble as they are associated with various psychiatric disorders, including depression, anxiety disorder, bipolar disorder, schizophrenia, and the dark triad disorders. For instance, low serotonin is often observed in the brains of people with major depressive disorder or anxiety disorder. Low serotonin could indicate too much MAO-A circulating in the brain. In fact, the first class of antidepressants used to treat such cases acted to specifically inhibit MAO-A, leading to increased levels of serotonin. MAOA (the gene), which codes for the enzyme, is located on the X chromosome. Since the 1990s, scientists have identified several versions of MAOA, which are usually categorized as low-activity or high-activity variants. MAOA genes are classified based on how many times a short sequence—a functional strip of DNA—repeats itself within a variable region of the gene. The most common variant, MAOA-4R, has four repeats and is associated with high-activity breakdown of neurotransmitters. Alternate forms of the MAOA, including the two-repeat (MAOA-2R) and three-repeat (MAOA-3R) versions, contain fewer repeat sequences and are associated with low-activity breakdown of neurotransmitters. The low-activity variants of the gene are particularly important for our topic, since they have been associated with aggressiveness and risk-taking. In fact, this association has earned low-activity MAOA the nickname of "the warrior gene."

The 2R variant, sometimes called the "extreme warrior gene," is a rare variant, as it is found in less than 1 percent of Caucasian American males and about 5 percent of African American males. It has been associated with an increase in the likelihood of committing serious crimes or violence. For instance, a recent analysis of a sample of males drawn from the National Longitudinal Study of Adolescent to Adult Health by Kevin Beaver and collaborators revealed that the extreme warrior gene was related to arrest, incarceration, and lifetime antisocial behavior among African American males. The 3R variant is associated with various degrees of aggression and risk-taking. It is the more prevalent form of the warrior gene, as it is found in roughly 35 percent of Caucasian males. The warrior gene is a recessive gene of the X chromosome. When present in males, it is always expressed, since males only have one X chromosome. In females, two copies are needed (one on each X chromosome) for the expression of the traits associated with the gene. What this means in practice is that, while roughly 35 percent of Caucasian men have a genetic propensity for aggression and risk-taking under certain environmental circumstances, only about 12 percent of Caucasian women have the same predisposition. For instance, in a 2012 study, Rose McDermott (from the department of political science at Brown University) and collaborators have found that individuals with the warrior gene who are exposed to violence in youth have a greater likelihood of engaging in physical aggression later in adulthood.

It should be noted that the propensity toward aggression and risk-taking involves a set of complex psychological traits that are not only manifested as a result of gene-environment interactions, but in all probability, also stem from the cumulative effect of multiple genetic contributions, of which the contribution from the warrior gene may be the most prominent. A very interesting study by Cary Frydman and collaborators revealed that carriers of the warrior gene were more likely to take financial risks than carriers of the high-activity variants of MAOA. More importantly, using a computational choice model rooted in established decision theory, they were able to show that carriers of the warrior gene exhibited such behavior because they are able to make *better* financial decisions under risk, and not because they are more impulsive. Indeed, they only took financial risk when it was advantageous to do so given their preferences over risk. For disadvantageous gambles, there was no difference between carriers of the warrior gene and carriers of the high-activity variant of MAOA. This suggests that the warrior gene carriers perform better when it comes to risky financial decision-making because they exhibit an improved ability to select the optimal response when it is advantageous. In light of these findings, if we take the portrait of the kind of person one would intuitively take to be power-oriented—hard-charging, competitive, impatient, aggressive, distrustful of others, and confident—a mix readily tied to Machiavellianism, and add the ability to make the cold, carefully calculated moves that Machiavellians are known for, it may be safe to assume that those individuals who are successful in their quest for power may have the warrior gene to thank for this, among other biological attributes. An interesting piece of future research would be one looking to confirm whether individuals presenting with dark triad traits are, indeed, more likely than the general population to have the warrior gene.

Machiavellianism lies in the midrange of the continuum of dark triad traits. Narcissism represents the lighter end of the spectrum, while psychopathy corresponds to the darkest, most extreme end. It is clear that the impulsive, callous, and often violent behaviors characteristic of extreme psychopaths are more likely to land them in prison than in the corner office. A study by Daniel Spurk, Anita Keller, and Andreas Hirschi analyzed incremental effects of single dark triad traits (i.e., narcissism, Machiavellianism, and psychopathy) on objective career success outcomes, such as salary and leadership position, and subjective career success outcomes, such as career satisfaction. The researchers analyzed 793 early career employees representative of age and education from the private industry sector in Germany. After controlling for other relevant variables such as gender, age, job tenure, organization size, education, and work hours, narcissism was found to be positively related to salary, Machiavellianism was positively related to leadership position and career satisfaction, and psychopathy was negatively related to all analyzed outcomes. The study lends support to the idea that both narcissistic and, even more strongly, Machiavellian traits may confer an advantage to those pursuing power.

Entrepreneurship is emblematic of risk-taking in the pursuit of power. Individuals choose careers and work environments that best fit their values, needs, and personalities. Narcissistic individuals are known to constantly fantasize about fame and power and see themselves as more intelligent and attractive than others. They are attracted to notoriety and tasks that support their superiority to others in a competitive way. In fact, not surprisingly, narcissists seem to seek out leadership positions in organizations. And what is a better position for leadership and power than owning a business? Indeed, some of the wealthiest people known today—Bill Gates, Warren Buffett, Jeff Bezos, among others—owe their success to entrepreneurship. All this lead Cynthia Mathieu and Étienne St-Jean (from the University of Quebec at Trois-Rivières) to surmise that entrepreneurship could attract individuals with greater narcissistic personality than other vocational choices. The idea seemed especially salient given that prior research had shown that entrepreneurs scored significantly higher than managers on risk propensity and many studies had linked high-risk propensity behaviors to narcissism. Given their display of overconfidence and, perhaps, the special appeal of power and success to them, narcissistic individuals may be more prone to risk-taking and differ from those who are not narcissistic in that they perceive greater benefits deriving from risky behaviors. Consequently, Mathieu and St-Jean designed a study to test whether entrepreneurs are more narcissistic than other vocational groups. Furthermore, their study measured the role of narcissism in explaining entrepreneurial intentions. Risk propensity, self-efficacy, and internal locus of control are the personality traits that have been most studied in relation to entrepreneurship, which is why they chose to specifically measure those traits in the people they included in their study.

Self-efficacy refers to the belief that an individual has it in his or her ability to accomplish specific tasks undertaken. One's perception of self-efficacy does not depend on the number of skills one possesses, but in the belief of what one is able to do with one's own skills in a variety of situations. Individuals who present high-generalized self-efficacy have higher hopes of success. High levels of generalized self-efficacy have also been associated with business creation. Narcissistic individuals have inflated views of their abilities and think that they are special and unique. Furthermore, even when faced with opposing facts, it seems that individuals high on narcissism still consider that they do better than others and predict that they would do better than others in similar tasks in the future. *Internal locus of control* refers to the belief that one is in control of one's own destiny. Entrepreneurs are by definition individuals who chose to control their careers by creating and managing their own business. Machiavellians, more than narcissists, tend to show high levels of internal locus of control. But we already discussed how the two sets of traits come on a continuum, meaning narcissists, too, tend to have above-average levels of internal locus of control. Given this extensive overlap between entrepreneurial and narcissistic traits, it is natural to assume that entrepreneurs may be more narcissistic than other vocational groups. Risk propensity and self-efficacy are the main drivers behind entrepreneurial intension. Low self-efficacy may explain entrepreneurial avoidance based on the fact that there may be individuals who avoid starting a business not because they lack the necessary skills, but because they think they do. On the contrary, if we look at narcissists who tend to have inflated views of their abilities, we could hypothesize that they would think they have the necessary skills to start a business (even though, in reality, they may not). Hence, narcissism may influence entrepreneurial intensions.

The data for the study came from 655 students who completed an initial online survey and took part in a six-month follow-up, in which several personality measures were included. Of these students, 108 had been entrepreneurs and seventy-three wanted to start a business in the future. The researchers also analyzed data from ninety-eight employees and managers from a large Canadian financial institution, who completed an online survey during work hours, and from 116 white-collar workers and managers working for a public organization. The study found that student entrepreneurs were more narcissistic than students who were not entrepreneurs, employees and managers from the financial institution, and workers from the public organization. Results also indicated that high scores on narcissism were positively associated with high scores on self-efficacy, internal locus of control, and risk propensity. In terms of predicting the intention to start a business, self-efficacy and risk propensity were good predictors, with risk propensity being the strongest predictor. In terms of sex, the study found that entrepreneurial intentions were significantly lower for women, which is in line with the general finding that more men than women present dark triad traits, including narcissistic traits.

Should these findings make someone who is low on dark triad tendencies give up hope of ever being entrepreneurial enough to achieve power? The answer is *no*. Firstly, dark triad traits are neither laudable nor desirable in general, and unless accompanied by a good dose of actual ability, labor, and luck, they are more likely to result in parasitism than in successful entrepreneurship. Secondly, there exist many ways to obtain power other than through business ownership. Lastly, genes are not destiny. If 50 percent of our traits are determined genetically, a whole other 50 percent are left to environment. The choices that we make in life matter. For instance, many people who carry the so-called "obesity genes" do not become overweight. Being aware of one's propensity for obesity and then choosing to eat a healthy diet and get enough exercise can help counteract some of the gene-related obesity risk. Evolution has acted so that genes and environment work to complement each other in yielding behavioral solutions to the survival challenges we may face.

Whilst some of us are genetically wired to seek power more avidly than others, having more control and power over our own lives and the world around us is desirable by all. If you have power, you can live life on your own terms, influence the behavior of others, get people to do what you want them to do, bring about change, and have an impact in the world. In fact, belief in one's ability to exert control over one's environment and produce desired results is essential for an individual's well-being. Specific behaviors can predict power, and many of them can be learned. Power rests with those who act, especially those who act with self-determination and persistence. Individuals with little experience in acting as an effective agent will likely have little belief in their ability to produce desired results, leading to feelings of helplessness and depression. Conversely, beliefs in one's abilities to exert control over one's environment and act as an agent capable of producing desired results will lead to a high sense of self-efficacy—and the stronger the perceived self-efficacy, the higher the goals people set for themselves, the better they perform at school, work, and personal relationships, and the happier they are. Our motivation is our most valuable commodity. Multiplied only by action, its value fluctuates with how we invest our attention. When we direct our focus toward achieving goals that are challenging, specific, and congruent with our sense of self, we give ourselves a chance to rise above our limitations and achieve a sense of power and control over our lives. Wandering among the dead and taking a closer look at the lives of those among them who got to enjoy a greater degree of power while alive reveals choices and strategies that they all used to varying degrees in their successful pursuit of power. Many of the power strategies catalogued by the likes of Niccolò Machiavelli and Baltasar Gracián are now being validated by science. Let's next delve into the ten must-know behavioral strategies for success in the power game.

III

What Behavior Can Do: The Ten Rules of Gaining Power and Influence

7

Rule One: Develop Expertise

Success results from a combination of innate ability, work, and luck. All three are required. Work is the only factor among the three that is amenable to control. It is also the skeleton key to the two others: without work, ability will remain undeveloped and lucky opportunities hidden. So control what you can control and put in the work. There is no real substitute for hard work, and it takes hard work and dedicated perseverance to convert talent into success. Mediocre people who apply themselves and persevere reach further heights than people of greater ability who do not. Practice makes perfect. Fortune is helped along by effort. Tiger Woods was not born a top golfer. It took sweat and toil to nurture his ability and perfect his game. No one is born to perfection. It takes focus and daily practice to round off one's gifts and reach eminence. Trust that lucky opportunities will show up along the way to help your effort. Good fortune does not just fall out of the sky; it is spotted along the effortful hike to perfection.

Society seems to have a default role for all. Unless you act, you will end up doing exactly what it expects you to do and being who it expects you to be. Do not let others foist an inferior image on you. Create your own. For much of human history, the ability to redefine oneself through art or science used to be the privilege of the aristocrats—more specifically, the males of the wealthiest class. The rest of mankind was confined to the limited role that society had predefined for them. Women were especially restricted, as they were strictly steered into motherhood and subjugation, regardless of social class. Even today, the girls who do not take their destiny into their own hands and put forth an effort to redefine themselves will end up in just the same spot: unfulfilling procreation and lifelong subjugation. It can be hard to know yourself when living in a culture that sends us constant messages about who we should be and what we should like. Begin by making choices for your life, instead of looking to others to make decisions for you. Question groupthink. Practice introspection. Read. Become more self-aware through trial and error. Use challenges as ways to test your limits. Over time, you may notice that acting in ways that fit with who you are simply feels better than acting in ways that do not naturally align with your true self. Continuing to set and meet goals will enable the belief that you are competent and capable. Be bold. Try out new things. Imitate the narcissists: believe in your superiority and affirm that you deserve better. With perseverance, your belief may just become a self-fulfilling prophecy.

Ignorance is rough and rude. It can kill the unsuspecting. Many do not know how their brains and bodies work, how they unconsciously generate their own reality, or what the obstacles to their success and happiness might be. They cannot even articulate their values and core beliefs, let alone improve and refine them for greater success in their lives. As a result, they end up living suboptimal and unhappy lives. They make unfortunate mistakes, which cost them peace of mind. They are unprepared to tackle life's challenges. They end up bouncing from failure to failure in their relationships, finances, careers, and health. The first step to get out of this cycle is awareness: admitting that we do not know what we do not know. This is actually a lot tougher to do than it sounds. Indeed, research shows that the less competent you are at something socially or intellectually, the more confident you will be in your abilities in that area. One reason may be what psychologists call the *fundamental attribution error*, our tendency to attribute poor outcomes to external factors or other people, rather than to lack of knowledge or competence in ourselves, in an effort protect our self-image. Another reason may be the lack of social comparison: compared with people who are experts in particular areas, people who are incompetent in those same areas are less able to identify the skills in others. This is because those who are most ignorant and incompetent have no standard to which they can compare their own knowledge and performance, and also because they rarely receive transparent feedback from others about their performance out of social tact or diplomacy. Even teachers are discouraged from giving their students objective feedback: they must tell all of them that they are heroes, lest they inflict permanent harm to their self-esteem. Furthermore, we tend to avoid the activities that we are not good at. This means that people who are incompetent in a specific area are not faced with their incompetence often, which gives them less opportunity to correct their errors, exacerbating the deficiencies. Finally, the halo effect may lead people who are actually skilled and experienced in a particular area to, mistakenly, believe that their skills and experience are transferable to other areas with which they are less familiar. Do your best to find an objective way to assess your expertise. Stop living on autopilot and start thinking about what you are doing and the consequences that can come with it. Train yourself to become more self-aware. Realizing a personal weakness will give you an opportunity to find ways to fix it. When it comes to knowing your competency level for a particular skill, nothing beats direct competition with those widely acclaimed for the skill. Learning by reading is the next best thing. For most of us, the more we learn, the more we realize how little we actually knew. When you realize that there are gaps in your knowledge of a topic, you may want to learn even more to fill in those gaps. And through practice and perseverance you will gain new skills and mastery.

Knowledge makes perfect. The first third of life should be spent learning as much as one can. It is even better to never stop learning. Beware, however, when you inform yourself about life. Only a small portion of our knowledge comes from direct experience, and much of it is relayed through others. One hundred individuals observing the same event will give one hundred different accounts of it. Facts are always filtered through emotions, resulting in various degrees of distortion. We all live in the same world, but we each have our own mental representation of it. Even science is often biased. Look for the same information from multiple sources and always subject it to scrutiny before accepting it for truth. Like the cynics, question people's motives and assume that they are acting self-servingly unless proven otherwise. It is the best way to guard yourself against spin and manipulation. Morality is seldom neutral. Before you declare yourself a moralist, make sure you clearly understand whose interests you are siding with, whom you are going against, and why. The questioning and doubt are not ends in themselves, but the means of blowing away the fog and confusion and seeing reality with lucidity and clarity. It is only by being distrustful that we can distinguish between the trustworthy and the unreliable, guard ourselves against the worst, and improve upon the substandard. Learning to think for oneself is the single greatest skill one can develop in life. Those who manage to master it are grounded and happy, and those who do not live in misery, as they always remain at the mercy of others.

Knowledge alone is not enough—one also needs to muster the courage to act. Without knowledge, you will remain in the dark. Without courage, wisdom can bear no fruit. As the saying goes, "Intelligence without ambition is like a bird without wings." Some individuals have impressive natural gifts and aptitudes, but do not have strong desires or motivations. So their true potential often remains unrealized. Your drive to accomplish something great is like the fuel needed to power the engine and propel a car forward. Without it, you will remain stuck in place. Whatever field you have chosen to pursue, pick a heroic model to emulate—someone who has accomplished great achievements in the same field. Your goal should not just be to follow this person's steps, but to eventually surpass them. The most successful people are also the ones who have failed the most. Failure should not scare you away from further trial and error. Risking big sometimes means losing big. Those who eventually triumph are the ones who know to pick themselves back up, dust themselves off, and move in another direction. As we learned previously, what does not kill us, sometimes, makes us stronger and more resilient.

Perfection is not quantity, but quality. It requires depth, rather than breadth. Specialization will lead to eminence and, when very few can excel at the task, even fame. The cardiac surgeon, a specialist, has far greater income than the family physician, a generalist—and, talent and opportunity permitting, a far better shot at fame, too. When it comes to selecting your professional degree, if you are more specialized, you will have a greater opportunity to differentiate yourself in the job marketplace. With specialization, advanced education or degrees are often needed. The best strategy is to accumulate as solid a general knowledge base as possible in youth and focus most of our later efforts on an ever-narrower field. The earlier years should also be the prime time to get to know our natural proclivities so that we can choose our field of specialization well. Nothing hurts more and wastes more time and effort than choosing to pursue the wrong profession. You know you have made that mistake when, despite years of heroic efforts, you can barely manage to reach mediocrity. It takes true courage to recognize it and even more courage to leave that field in order to start over in a different one that may be a better personal fit. Work and perseverance are necessary, but they can never beat genetics. The key is to specialize in a profession that best fits our genetic selves.

Be realistic about yourself. Most people overestimate their abilities. Unrealistic optimism is an innate human tendency to protect us against depression and keep us motivated. For instance, when people think about the future, they tend to underestimate their chances of developing cancer, getting a divorce, or being involved in a car crash. They also think of themselves as more virtuous, more talented, and more empathetic than others. Conversely, people with depression make more accurate judgements and realistic predictions than people without depression. For instance, when asked to assess their own performance in a novel task and in the absence of feedback, people with depression are more likely to assess their performance accurately than those without depression. It is a good idea to aim a little high, but not so high as to miss the mark. One only has a chance at excellence when one aims within one's true capabilities. Our brains are pattern-matching machines, and the closer a situation is to one we have previously experienced, the better it is at calibrating our expectations. It is notoriously bad at guessing how we may feel or how we may perform in an entirely new scenario. So want the best, but expect the worst, so that you may accept the outcome without too deep a disillusionment. When you start your first job, temper your imagination. Go into it with courage, prudence, and the intention to put forth a good-faith effort. Then take a wait-and-see approach. Excessive disappointment can dampen courage and lead to learned helplessness. You will need to keep your head up and muster the courage to move on should you fail.

When you are a beginner, stick to what is tried-and-true in your profession. Those who know little should use the main highway. Keep it simple. Repeat. As your knowledge widens, you can afford to go sideways and try new routes. Asking for advice from your more experienced colleagues will not cast doubt on your talent. They have been where you are now and know how it feels. Most will feel respected and flattered when asked for counsel by a junior colleague and will happily give it to you. Better to ask and do it right than remain in the dark and do it all wrong. Do not be afraid of "stealing" their ideas—we all steal ideas from each other. Why waste time trying to reinvent the wheel? Innovation does not necessarily involve an entirely novel concept, process, or product. Entrepreneurs can take an existing product or technology and create something completely new out of it by repurposing it for a different market or use than what it was originally intended for. So inform yourself and, whenever possible, use the existing blueprint.

Do not dwell on difficulties, as that will lead to discouragement. When confronted with a particularly difficult task, undertake it as though it were easy. Do not overthink it. Worrying about certain outcomes, which may not even happen, can paralyze us. Overthinking creates so many options, choices, and scenarios that you may end up becoming unable to make a decision. Sometimes it is enough to just take action. Many successful entrepreneurs will tell you that, starting out, they had little clue about how to turn their dreams into reality. They just jumped off the cliff and figured out a way to build a parachute on the way down. If you put an animal in danger, it will figure out a way to adapt and survive. Too much anxiety can make you miserable and mentally exhausted, and even cause depression. Conversely, undertake easy tasks as though they were difficult. This will avoid the mistakes that often stem from overconfidence.

Some people promise much and deliver little. They build impressive castles out of thin air. Unfounded things never reach old age. When their ghastly construction finally comes tumbling down, their reputation is irredeemably ruined. A person of substance knows to utter the right words, but also makes sure to follow through with the right deeds. It is easy to speak and difficult to act. Be a doer and leave the talking to others. It is better to underpromise and overdeliver than to set others' expectations high and disappoint. Reputations based on substance are the only enduring kind. You buy your reputation with your hard work and merit. It is an expensive thing. Know how to build it but, even more importantly, know how to keep it once you have made it.

It is not enough to be intelligent, you must also develop the right character. Following tasks through to completion, backing up your fine words with solid deeds, excelling at some lofty pursuit, and keeping your head up in the face of adversity are all parts of developing a character worthy of respect. Temperament is inherited. Character builds on temperament through experience and learning. It pays to become aware of one's defects and ameliorate them to achieve superior character. There is nothing better for such awareness than a sharp criticism from an opponent. Know to put your enemies to good use. The acidic words of an enemy often contain more truth than the sweet flatteries of a friend. Let go of your emotions and see the truth behind the aggression. Rather than being offended by their frank words, take them as advice to improve yourself.

In the state of nature, we are no better than beasts. Feral children are proof enough. Culture raises us above our base instincts. Knowledge is the ultimate way to build culture. But knowledge alone is coarse when polish is lacking. We must refine not only our understanding, but also our desires and our conversation. Elegant and graceful people show proper etiquette: they dress tastefully, speak with confidence, converse with charm, and act with courtesy, dignity, and poise. Impeccable manners and the ability to move with ease and grace in the social arena are key characteristics of powerful, successful people—in business and social life. Nothing helps in the way of developing such refinement than the company of others, especially those of superior wisdom, taste, and manners. Leave your envy at the door. Feel fortunate to be allowed in their company, observe them, and learn from them.

Knowing how to skillfully use artifice is a sign of refinement. Some situations require it. It differs from fraud in that it is not motivated by malevolence, but by honorable intentions. When strength lacks, one can resort to skill. Some rules, when applied too literally or too systematically, do more harm than good. It takes courage and subtlety to circle around them skillfully. Sometimes a harmless white lie is the best course of action. Some laws are specifically designed to harm innocent people—any laws that forbid women from owning property or holding a job are glaring examples. Such laws deserve to be broken—until they are repealed—but in a subtle enough way that one does not get caught or punished. It takes superior intelligence, extreme courage, and a refined character to live the life of Susan B. Anthony in the thick of the nineteenth century.

Inventiveness often stems from exceptional intelligence. It is what allows us to be the first at spelling out a novel idea, gaining a new understanding, building a never-before-built machine, or improving an existing process. It is excellence at its acme, as those who follow will never be able to shake the accusation that they are mere imitators. The bigger the invention, the bigger the fortune, and the more enduring the fame. The dilemma of all creative geniuses has always been, however, the danger of slipping into madness. Mental illness has both the fortunate and unfortunate effect of weakening the control normally exerted by our prefrontal cortex over the rest of the brain. When ideas are allowed to fly freely and brain areas that typically function distinctly start to communicate with one another, concepts that previously seemed unrelated can be tied together, resulting in something new. Whilst this process mostly produces garbage—as in the unintelligible word salad of a schizophrenic—in the rare cases where the brain is also endowed with acute intelligence, it can yield a beneficial discovery. It seems safer, albeit more mundane, to simply think well, reason well, and have pleasant taste.

Do not get lulled into a sense of complacency. Complacency—that sense of quiet pleasure or security, usually accompanied by a lack of awareness of potential dangers or deficiencies, or that feeling of calm satisfaction with your own abilities or a situation that prevents you from trying harder—is the enemy of excellence and can lead to massive failure. The military has adopted the mantra that "complacency kills." As Murphy's Law is famously paraphrased, "Anything that can go wrong, will go wrong." If you have lived the same basic existence for years on end, you may have come to believe that you have experienced pretty much every scenario and can reliably predict the outcome of most situations. When we believe we know the answers, our creativity and ability to proactively plan for potential threats become stagnant. Things depend on circumstance. Sometimes they prevail, sometimes they fail. Even small probability events can happen if the dice are thrown enough times. A big win can induce overconfidence, which can border on outright arrogance. Stop pushing yourself to achieve new goals at work and you may be passed for the next promotion, if not downright demoted or fired. Become a bit too comfortable in your intimate relationship and your partner may feel neglected enough to break it off. What goes up must surely come down. Vigilance is the best antidote against complacency.

Being driven and focused, working hard, and persevering in the face of adversity are the core qualities that lead to eminence when coupled to true innate ability and some good luck. Excellence can have an invisible cost, however, paid in biological currency. Never neglect your health in your zeal to achieve perfection. It is often when we lose our health that we truly start to appreciate it. If you have an able body, it is the most precious asset you will ever have. Make a conscious effort to live a healthy lifestyle at all times. Eat a Mediterranean diet, exercise regularly, sleep for seven to eight hours daily, and manage stress through meditation or yoga. Nothing beats strength training in helping to prevent the natural loss of lean muscle mass that comes with aging (the medical term for this loss is *sarcopenia*). Strength training also increases bone density and reduces the risk of fractures. This, in turn, improves your quality of life and reduces your risk from falls and injuries. Since osteoporosis affects older women more often than older men, activities like walking or aerobics are especially important for women transitioning into menopause. Indeed, bone loss accelerates substantially in late perimenopause and continues at a similar pace in the first postmenopausal years. If exercise came in the form of a pill, it would be the most frequently prescribed medicine. It improves both body and brain function and boosts mood. Exercise is the best defense and repair strategy that we have to counter the deleterious effects of aging. Do not neglect to take an occasional vacation to relax and disconnect. Travel to enjoy novel experiences and make great memories. Have friends. Have lovers. Life is short. Health is precious. Nothing matters when it is lost. Guard it zealously.

8

Rule Two: Put Your Talent on Display

What is invisible might as well not exist. Excellence itself is not enough. All your skills and talents are worthless if you do not know how to sell yourself to others. Whether you are trying to get a job, push a start-up business, make new friends, or ask someone on a date, the ultimate end goal is to win people over. Selling yourself means communicating your value to others. Put your gifts on display, but learn to show them off with skill. You have to find a delicate balance between confidence in your ability to handle a particular situation and the humility to show others that you need their help in order for your goal to reach its true potential. You also have to find a balance between showcasing your best talents without cheapening them. The key is to communicate your value not only in terms of your own interests, but also in terms of how it can meet the needs of others and illustrate how they can benefit from the unique value you bring to the table. When you have talent, but no talent for displaying it, you risk not going very far. Many academics with prodigious talent fail to secure a university career because they have little skill at selling their ideas, however excellent they may be. Deceit is rampant and things are seldom what they seem. An inferior, but well-worded idea will, sometimes, steal the grant money that might have otherwise funded a superior, but poorly formulated one. This matters tremendously, because for a junior professor, a single grant can make or break a whole career. A good salesperson knows how to artfully spin ideas and will emphasize the benefits of a product to a prospective customer over the features of said product. People are not so much interested in what is in it for you as in what is in it for them. It is simply a fact that personal context is usually the first filter we use to evaluate our environment. To earn business or get compliance, learn to word your requests in terms of others' interests. Adapt your value proposition to circumstance. Put your talent in plain view when the time is ripe. Ostentation will seem vulgar and pretentious when done out of season. Show discernment and patience. Beware excess in your display. Do it in moderation, revealing a little more over time. It is good to be intelligent, but not to be pedantic. Give too much advice and you risk being perceived as overbearing. Too much of a good thing can be a bad thing.

Not everyone looks at substance. In fact, most people stop at appearance. Attraction is key when it comes to earning respect from others. Your appearance is a reflection of your own self-esteem. Nobody is going to respect someone who does not look like they respect themselves. The effects of first impressions are hard to undo. People will very quickly make assumptions based on your personal appearance, including your facial expressions, the clothes you wear, whether you are groomed well, and your body language. A person with a clean, hygienic look will always be associated with positive traits, such as trustworthiness, dependability, and sociability, and will be treated accordingly. Although your appearance and fashion sense are not objectively correlated to your job skills, a professional appearance shows that you are able to put up a respectable work ethic. Dress tastefully and appropriately for the occasion, but dress to impress. If you want a promotion, dress like the person above you. Maintain proper posture. Impeccable hygiene is not just a health requirement, it is a social obligation. Speak well. Use proper grammar. Enrich your vocabulary. Impeccable language is not a luxury, but a necessity. Do not gossip. Always try to find something to praise about others. Be pleasant and amicable. Speak with confidence. Make eye contact. Look like you are contributing something valuable. As Baltasar Gracián put it, "A fine exterior is the best adornment for inner perfection."

Express your ideas with lucidity, but not with excessive clarity. Lucidity shows that you know what you are talking about. Your ideas should be intelligible enough, but not inordinately so. It is good to be somewhat obscure so as not to seem vulgar. Many do not really understand why they acclaim someone. They do so because they hear others do it. When a person is in a situation where they are unsure of the correct way to behave or think, they will often look to others for clues concerning the correct behavior or thought. Uncertainty is a major factor that encourages the use of social proof. We conform with the majority under uncertainty because we believe that others' interpretation of an ambiguous situation is more accurate than ours and will help us choose an appropriate course of action or thought. The confused have sometimes been venerated for being mysterious. Even if you are saying something banal, it will seem original if you make it sound vague enough.

When you are trying to impress people with words, the more you say, the more likely you are to say something foolish. If others understand you too clearly, you risk losing their respect. Most people think little of what they understand and venerate what they do not. If you say little, they will fill the uncomfortable void with imaginings of their own. Andy Warhol is famous for saying as little as possible about his work and letting others do all the interpreting. We all have a habit of talking our way out of success, money, and good fortune—unintentionally—by talking too much. The following quote, which Robert Greene attributes to Leonardo da Vinci, illustrates this point by way of an amusing metaphor: "Oysters open completely when the moon is full; and when the crab sees one it throws a piece of stone or seaweed into it and the oyster cannot close again so it serves the crab for meat. Such is the fate of him who opens his mouth too much and thereby puts himself at the mercy of his listener." When you speak, say less—leaving your listener not only pondering the words that were spoken, but also the words that were not.

The more effortful your displays, the less talented you will seem. Ease and grace are signs of natural gifts. Many dancers have improved their performance with practice and have mastered the techniques to an extent that they are technically brilliant. Few, however, have a certain ineffable lightness and otherworldliness in their movements, an intuitive awareness, and grace that shows how they can easily create beauty through their bodies. At the sight of their elegance, you are forced to think that, maybe, it all stems from an inborn talent. Structured training, practice, dedication, discipline, hard work, and motivation might have been sine qua non for their talent to be developed and noticed. But they seem to have gone further, with more ease than most of their peers trained with the same rigor. Work can add but an infinitesimal amount above and beyond fully tapped natural ability. Those who struggle too much lack ability. Putting your effort where you have the most natural gifts does not just give you the best shot at eminence, it also gives you the best shot at displaying your talent advantageously. The better you are at something, the more you should hide your efforts, so that perfection seems to occur naturally.

Do not show half-finished things to others. Only present them in their finished perfection. Like planets at birth, all beginnings are formless. Show your art early, and its lingering deformity will distract from its final perfection. The effect of the negative first impression will taint its finished beauty for eternity. Displaying too many incomplete projects will also cast a shadow on your character. Having a house full of half-completed projects is a hallmark of bipolar disorder. Those, among the afflicted, who can harness their energy when they are in a hypomanic phase, can be very productive. Those who cannot, however, often go from task to task, planning grand, unrealistic projects that are never finished before moving on to something else. If people do not go so far as to assume that you have bipolar disorder, they can, at the very least, assume that you are fickle and unreliable. Finish up your art, complete your project, give form to your idea, and, then, let others enjoy them in their finalized perfection.

People will be more likely to believe in your talent when you believe in it yourself. In a perfect world, people would be able to gauge your talents with great accuracy, so that you would not need to engage in any form of self-promotion. But talents can be notoriously hard to judge. Talent can be elusive because it is quite easy to fake, especially when people are deluded about their own capabilities. The proof is that narcissists and psychopaths can nail a job interview like no one else can. Indeed, fooling others is much easier when you have managed to fool yourself beforehand. Extraversion can easily pass for social skill, confidence for competence, and charisma for leadership potential. When you have actual talent, it is a shame that it should go unnoticed for lack of confidence. Projecting confidence will help you gain credibility, make a strong first impression, deal with pressure, and tackle personal and professional challenges. It is also an attractive trait, as confidence helps put others at ease. Confidence can be developed by practicing in social settings and from personal and professional accomplishments. The more goals you set up for yourself and meet, the stronger your belief in your own competence and capability will grow. Self-doubt is off-putting. People can smell weakness, and most people resent it. Maintain a healthy dose of respect for yourself. Walk into a room with your head held high. Make sure you come across as grounded and confident in your interactions with others.

Always make those above you feel comfortably superior. Whatever you do, do not appear smarter than your boss. A newbie to management may especially fear that their employee will upstage them. In your desire to please and impress them, do not go too far in displaying your talents or you might accomplish the opposite—inspiring fear and insecurity. Do not badmouth your boss; it will work against you. Instead of whining about what your boss lacks, do what you can to fill in those gaps. Be genuinely helpful. Make your boss look good. There is no reason not to be generous. Looking good is not a zero-sum game. Being perceived to be a strong and effective leader will help with your boss's own career, and you will have an influential person on your side when you need it. In a large corporate environment, part of your reputation is based on the people around you. If you are within a successful team, you can use this success to your advantage when you are up for promotion or a transfer to another part of the company. Making those above you look good will make them like you, which will surely help avoid their wrath and earn their trust, and maybe even give you a leg up for when the next big project comes up that everyone wants. Be genuine in your praise and your help. If your support is more about posturing, it can easily backfire. Making your boss look good should be effortless and flow with opportunities as they present themselves. If you are working too hard at making your boss look good, you may be compromising both your values and your reputation.

Always leave room for imagination when displaying your talent. Show it partially and leave people expecting more. Use the halo effect of a good deed. When others see you excel under a difficult circumstance, they will automatically assume that you might excel under other tenuous conditions. It is an inborn bias of the human brain. They cannot help it. Do it twice, and they will be fully convinced of your brilliance. If they do not know the true extent of your abilities, they will not be disappointed. Many admire what they do not know or understand. Use this tendency to your advantage.

Use the scarcity heuristic to stoke people's desire and esteem. The scarcity heuristic stems from the idea that the more difficult it is to acquire an item, the more value that item has. Simply put, humans have an innate tendency to place a higher value on things that are scarce and a lower value on those that are found in abundance. Savvy marketers routinely use the scarcity bias to their advantage in their advertising messages by telling customers that certain goods will sell out quickly, making a limited-time offer, or by using limited editions to constrain the production of an item. Scarcity is paramount for luxury brands, because at the root of the very notion of luxury, supply must never outgrow demand. The reason that scarcity messages trigger us is that we want to possess the things that only a select number of others have. We do that in an attempt to increase our social status, reduce the feeling of powerlessness, and generate envy. Scarcity can have a big influence on our perception of the attractiveness and worth of someone else. Never share too much about yourself. Excessive familiarity tends to breed contempt. Keep a healthy dose of distance between you and others, even friends. Being too present will also diminish respect. Use strategic absence to win esteem. Making your assistance too readily available will only cheapen it. Scarcity is what drives up the price of a valuable skill. This comes down to economics—if your skill is in low supply and high demand, it is worth more. It is easy to become excited when an unexpected professional opportunity presents itself, but remember that your power in any negotiation comes from your ability to walk away. When you worry about all the things you may lose out on if you do not eagerly take a particular opportunity, you may come across as desperate and cheapen the perceived value of what you bring to the table. Adopt an abundance mindset instead. Recognizing that there are unlimited possibilities can give you the security and confidence you need to create successful outcomes. Play hard to get. Believe in your uniqueness. Demand more and you may just get more.

Merit alone is not enough, you must also please others. A good salesperson knows that people buy from you because they like you. Be polite and charming to win people over. When you first meet someone, repeat the sweetest sound in the world—their name—to remember it, and then drop it occasionally into the conversation. No matter what they tell you, people are always only interested in themselves, not you. Show genuine interest in them, retain eye contact, and ask questions. If you are asked a question, keep things short and sweet, be humble, do not show off, and do not bring up anything negative, political, or inappropriate. Make sure to exude confidence in your posture, tone of voice, language, and mannerisms. Only talk positively about others. People rarely like backstabbers. Everyone loves a happy person, so smile and be glad to be around others. Your charm and courtesy will win the goodwill of others and, also, their business and benevolence.

9

Rule Three: Sharpen Your Time-Management Skills

Time management is the process of planning and exercising conscious control over the time spent on specific activities in order to work smarter, rather than harder, so that you get more done in less time, even when time is tight and pressures are high. Effective time management in the workplace means meeting important goals on time, delivering quality work, being more productive, reducing the stress and anxiety that can come with procrastination, better work-life balance, and ultimately a happier life. When we fill our time with little things that are not important, we leave little time to take care of the things that actually matter. Imagine trying to fit big rocks, pebbles, and sand into an empty jar. You will not have room for the big rocks if you start filling the jar by first adding sand, then the pebbles. If you start by adding the big rocks first, however, the pebbles and sand will elegantly fit into the spaces left between the rocks. The big rocks symbolize the things that are the most important in your workload. The pebbles represent everything of medium importance, while the sand represents all of the smaller items that are less important in your work. Do the essential things first, and later, if there is time, those that are secondary. When you learn to take control of your time on a daily basis, you improve your ability to get things done, make better decisions, and, most importantly, gain ultimate control over your key priorities. Effective time management is of the essence. It requires that we identify the tasks at hand, prioritize them, and make time blocks on our calendar for the most important items. The rest will fit in where they may.

What applies to our daily work schedule also applies to our lives. Some people delay their big dreams and spend their youthful years on learning less glamorous and more practical skills. If you postpone what might bring renown until the end of your life, you might well end up postponing it until afterlife, assuming that such a thing exists at all. Some rest at the beginning of life and leave effort for last. Then, they are surprised to realize that their old bones will not sustain the workload. The only solace they can find for their misfortune in life is to blame it on others or external circumstances. Some people abandon the effort as soon as they have begun to make their fortune and are astounded when the good times come to an end. Take charge of your life and, even more importantly, take responsibility for your failures. If you do not make your goals happen, nobody else will do it for you. Planning, prioritizing, and persevering are as essential to living as they are to learning and working.

It is worse to busy yourself with the trivial than to do nothing. Certain easy and mechanical tasks need to be done daily and take up precious time. Find a way to delegate them. Unless you intend to become a celebrity chef yourself, let those who work at restaurants cook your food, serve it, and take care of the dishes, instead of doing all of that yourself day in and day out. Paying for daycare may be worth every single penny in the long run. Have your house professionally cleaned. If you can afford it, do not do it yourself. Specialization yields best results. The right kind of leisure is better than the wrong kind of work. Time is precious given that life is so short. We can only do so much ourselves without being burnt out. Learn to delegate. The tasks that you enjoy doing, those with a high payoff, and those that carry the most potential for self-development should be yours to keep. Those you do not care for, find painful, or those with little payoff are ideal candidates to delegate to someone else. Certain complex tasks require many specialized skills to reach completion. Find people with the creativity and skills you lack. Do your research, hire the best, and pay them well. Coordinate their work, give them their due, and take credit for the end result. This is not immoral—it is part of the contract. Your time is better spent on developing yourself, perfecting your talents, and pursuing rewarding opportunities. And never neglect to enjoy life while you do so.

Weigh your personal matters carefully. Think hardest about those that matter the most. Much time is wasted by not thinking things through. Thinking is the precursor to all effective action and behavior, the only way to sort fact from fiction and truth from lies, the only way to guard ourselves against manipulation and costly mistakes, the only way to invent, plan, set and achieve goals, and ultimately the only way to a happy and healthy life. When confronted with multiple options, take the time to evaluate the pros and cons of each. Conduct proper due diligence before heading into a costly venture. The more important the problem and the bigger the impact of our decisions, the more we should be thinking things through before finalizing our choices. A marriage is the most expensive social contract most people will ever enter into. Many are clueless about its legal implications until a divorce comes along. Diligently consider all the costs, benefits, and risks. Thinking things through is harder than sweeping issues under the rug. However, dodging problems carries a price tag. Not only will you feel burdened by unresolved conflicts, you will probably keep repeating the same problem. We learn a lot throughout the course of a day, but if we do not take the time to reflect on what we learn, then a lot of that information gets misused or forgotten. Thinking your way through problems is a valuable way of finding solutions. But too much thinking can sometimes exacerbate problems. While it is at times appropriate to ruminate on an issue in our life until it is resolved, other times it is best to let go of reoccurring thoughts and move on, lest we slip into anxiety and depression. The key is to find a balance that works.

Choose your battles carefully. Some problems start out innocently, only to snowball into something much bigger. It would have been easy to put an end to them at the beginning. Early inaction ends up leading to a much costlier outcome later on. What is good enough, on the other hand, may be best left alone. Not everything can or should be perfect. Sometimes the cure is worse than the disease, and meddling can cause more problems than attempting to fix the disorder. Some issues are complex and intractable. Any hope of an immediate solution is futile. Such problems, sometimes, have a way of correcting themselves over time, and it may be best to ignore them for the moment. Do not get caught up in a circle of anxiety about every bothersome event. Few are important enough to be bothered with. Retiring to a safe harbor for a while to regain perspective can help. It can also help to consult someone with no emotional stake in the matter. Sometimes life happens, and there really is not a whole lot to be done besides accepting the facts and moving on. Try not to get caught up emotionally in such circumstances. When it comes to knowing the issues worth fixing from those best left alone, it pays to have life experience or seek the counsel of someone who does.

If you do not know where you are going, chances are you will end up someplace else. So plan ahead. Long-range plans rarely work exactly as they were laid out, but they are still essential. You can always adjust as circumstances change or new information becomes available. Oftentimes, small business owners and executives of growing organizations flounder because they do not have a plan, so they figure things out confusedly in the rush of events. Foresight might have prevented much frustration and, ultimately, failure. What is true for running a business is true for running your life. Your whole life should be a matter of thinking about your next destination.

Choosing the right profession to pursue is the single most important choice you will make in life. So choose wisely. It will spare you much grief and a lot of precious time. Know where you have the most ability. This lies in what comes easiest to you and difficult to others. When winning comes out of little effort, working will feel like a pleasurable hobby. Many would have achieved eminence if only they had known what they excelled at. Choose a celebrated occupation within the realm of what is achievable with your best ability. The most thankless occupation is one that is repetitive, takes over your whole person, and offers no room for personal or professional growth. Choose one in which there is ample room for growth. Society has set a price for what it judges every occupation to be worth. Some occupations are important, but they are barely visible. Choose a profession which is not just likely to bring higher esteem and lifetime earnings, but also best fits your genetic proclivities.

Stop being a people pleaser and learn how to confidently say *no* to somebody without feeling bad about it. As social beings, we are driven to preserve our relationships. It can be difficult to let people down, even if it is the right thing for you to do. The principle of reciprocity is a hardwired impulse. We fear losing the other person's future help if we do not help them now. Although we are also preprogrammed to want people to like us, to be popular, and to gain the approval of others, as modern humans, we are sophisticated enough to recognize that we should not be worried about what others think all of the time. It takes some skill to say *no* politely, but firmly. Keep it short. Do not give an explanation. No matter what excuse you offer, people who are determined to get you to say *yes* can come up with a way to invalidate it. Sometimes you can lessen the impact of your *no* by offering an alternative that satisfies their want, while being something that is more preferable to you. Perhaps you can refer them to someone else or offer partial help. If you always put other people's needs ahead of your own, you will find that your productivity will suffer and your resentment will mount. Saying *yes* is a time commitment. It takes time away from the things you want to do and the pleasures that give your life meaning. Overcommitment also risks damaging your reputation. If you let people down in the end or become known as someone with hollow promises, people will stop trusting you. Perhaps we can all learn from Warren Buffett, who summed it up in the following way: "The difference between successful people and very successful people is that very successful people say *no* to almost everything." It means saying *no* over and over again to the unimportant things flying in our direction every day and remaining focused on saying *yes* to the few things that truly matter.

Baltasar Gracián advised: "Never compete with someone who has nothing to lose." Take this advice to heart. A person who has nothing to lose has no fear and no shame. Unencumbered by the downside of trying, they are free from the inhibitions and anxieties that burden others with the possibility of failure or loss. If you have nothing to lose, the only option that remains is that anything you do, if it does not leave you in the status quo, will make you win. You can literally afford all risks. Any good general knows that if you put your soldiers into an inescapable situation, they will fight to the bitter end. Courage is often born out of sheer desperation. This is a time-tested offensive war stratagem to ensure victory. Beginners often have little to lose and sometimes try to win fame indirectly by cunningly opposing the greats in their field. The established and acclaimed should take guard. Their reputation took many years and much effort to build. They should not risk losing in it in an instant by taking the vulgar bait from such people. Indifference should reduce them to the oblivion they rightly deserve. Many people would be unknown if their excellent opponents had paid them no heed.

Do not multitask. It inhibits productivity. The human brain can only effectively concentrate on one task at a time. What multitaskers really do is quickly shift their attention and focus from one thing to the next. Trying to do more than one thing at a time—especially anything potentially dangerous, like texting while driving—seriously compromises our ability to complete the tasks safely and well. It makes it more difficult to tune out distractions, lowers productivity, and makes us more prone to making mistakes. If you try to do a few things at once, you never really focus on anything or deeply connect with others—be it your coworkers, customers, friends, or family. Multitasking increases stress and anxiety and taxes short-term memory. When we are anxious, our bodies start accessing more primitive brain structures that are designed to keep us safe from danger. When that happens, we stop accessing other areas, such as the prefrontal cortex, which has been evolved to serve the functions of critical thinking and creativity. When you distractedly attempt to complete small tasks while also trying to complete a large one, you will soon see how they actually eat up more of your time, rather than saving it. The mind has to reset to each task following the shift. Considering all of these reasons, it is easy to see why the power of multitasking is a myth that has never actually helped anybody to efficiently accomplish anything that matters. Instead, do one task at a time. Create more structure to your work.

Plan ahead and make time blocks in your calendar for your important tasks. Perform highly creative tasks in the morning, and then take a short break before moving on to each different task. By prioritizing and focusing on one task at a time, you will not only be more productive, but you will also enjoy each task more.

Do not dwell on the past. Learn from it, and then move on. We all make mistakes—some big, some small. What is done is done. Being stuck in regret is nonsensical self-flagellation, and it can be incredibly damaging to your mental health. The anxious and depressed are particularly known for ruminating endlessly about past events. Dwelling on regret is exhausting—it sucks all joy and fulfillment from your days and leaves you stuck, always looking backwards and unable to move forward in life. Look at the wider context in which you took the action causing your regret and understand why you took the path you did based on the information you had at the time. There is a tendency with regret to see the pathway you did not take as inevitably better than the pathway you did. It may well be that this other pathway would indeed have worked out better—but there is no way to know for sure. Regret is a tremendously useful feeling. Without regret, we cannot learn from our mistakes and we are destined to repeat them. Acknowledge the feeling, analyze it, and learn from it. View regret as an opportunity to do things differently next time, rather than a signal that you should give up trying altogether. Regret, although painful, can be a gift. It can be the doorway to a better way of living.

10

Rule Four: Associate with the Right People

Emotional states are contagious. One can catch both the happiness of the fortunate and the misery of the unfortunate. So associate with the fortunate and avoid the unfortunate. Upbeat emotions, such as enthusiasm, hope, and joy, as well as negative ones, such as sadness, fear, and anger, are easily passed from one person to another, often without either party realizing it. Humans, like other animals, are built to mimic one another unconsciously. This mimicry is the very basis of empathy. Upon seeing the facial and bodily expressions of another person, the mirror neurons of our brains trigger the activation of muscle fibers in our face and body, at levels far lower than if we were to perform those movements ourselves. These muscle movements then trigger the actual feelings that the other person is transmitting to us. Over time, this emotional contagion leads to the formation of social networks, where happy people find themselves in clusters of other happy people and unhappy people gather in unhappy clusters. Become aware of the emotions you exude toward others that they might pick up and of those that others exude that you are picking up. Then create change so that you end up in happy clusters.

Have friends. Life is flavorless without them. Friends can help bring out the best in you without expecting perfection. They can lift you up when you are feeling down. They can remind you not to take life too seriously when the going gets tough. Great friends can not only lift the quality of your life, but perhaps even the length of it. Indeed, close friendships can help ward off depression and boost immunity as well. Friendship involves giving and taking. Never forget that it is a two-way street. To have great friends, you first have to be one yourself. So be sure to boost your friends' self-confidence when they are feeling discouraged and be there for them when they need it. A great lover will do everything that a great friend will do, and even more. Make new friends every day. Find a good lover and treat them well. Chronic loneliness can kill. Once lonely, humans can get trapped in a psychological downward cycle from which it can be difficult to escape. Isolation can feed off of itself through selective attention to negative cues and social threat from others or the expectation of being socially excluded. In moments of uncertainty and danger, fight the natural human desire to run inward and isolate yourself. Having a good lover and a circle of close friends is oftentimes the best thing you can do for your happiness and health.

Select your friends. You will be judged by the friends you have. The people you associate with have a major impact on your personal success. They often influence how you feel, think, and behave. Associate higher. If you are running low on self-control, then seek out self-disciplined people to boost your willpower. If you want to get to the next socioeconomic level, choose those who are already there. If your taste is lacking, find a bon vivant to help you cultivate and refine it. Associate with those whom you can learn from. Well-read and well-travelled friends are not just great conversationalists, they make great teachers too. There are people of a cheerful disposition and vivid intelligence who attract happiness and prosperity unto themselves. They are a source of pleasure to those around them. Associate with them to share in the good fortune they draw upon themselves.

Contrary to myth, all human relationships come with an expiration date. Your good memories are precious. Protect them. Clinging to a soured relationship will only tarnish the memory of the good times you enjoyed with someone. Sometimes friends drift apart, whether you have less in common or life circumstances have changed. Envy can quickly poison a relationship when one friend stagnates or suffers a major setback in life, while the other one climbs up socially, economically, or professionally—especially if fortune strikes fast. When you are ambitious and talented, it only makes sense to refresh your circle of relationships periodically as you climb up the social ladder. If your friends are subtracting more from your life than they are adding to it, or if they are making you feel worse rather than better when you are with them, it may be time to cut ties. It is incredibly hard to cut off a friend, but keeping a toxic friend around is draining. In the long run, it is better to cut ties and find people who appreciate and support you. This rule applies to any person in your social circle, not just to friends. Whether you are dealing with a manipulative boss, an envious coworker, an insecure lover, or a pessimistic family member, toxic people can show up in everybody's lives. From causing extreme stress to slowing your progress, they can be a massive drain on your time, health, happiness, and even finances. Being a blood relative does not give a family member a free pass to be toxic at will. Many negative personal situations can be improved by simply creating space. When you see or talk to the person who brings negativity into your life less often, you will remove yourself from their dynamic and stop fanning the flames. Over time, all communication may naturally come to an end, sparing you an unpleasant confrontation and all the ill will it may cause.

Do not keep company with those who will make you seem less gifted, either because they are significantly superior or inferior. Associating with people who have little talent and little potential will only bring you disrepute, as others will rank you according to the company you keep. When you are starting out, you may not have much in the way of actual accomplishments, but people can sense potential in the naturally gifted. On your way up, associate with the great and work to make them look even better. The benefit of their teachings and connections will make up for the humiliation of being in their shadow for a while. Humility is a sign of prudence when one is starting out—if you remain there for too long, however, you will get little attention and little esteem, as the other person will always get the leading part. Once you have grown, step out of their shadow. Associate with people who are average instead. They will make you look so much better by comparison.

Your sympathy for the unfortunate can turn you into one of them. Time and again, upon seeing a drowning person in distress, people try to help and end up drowning themselves. Oftentimes, the water is calm, but the distressed person is so panicked that they grab onto the person trying to help them, and both succumb. Contact is what results in death. It would have been better to wait for professional help if you did not have a flotation device to use. Airlines advise us to place an oxygen mask over our own mouth and nose before helping others, even our children, should the cabin lose pressure. So help yourself first before helping others. To give something, one must first have something—preferably in excess quantity. Do not let others' misery drag you down. One cannot run a marathon if one is chained to an anchor. Do not feel bad for being ruthlessly selfish as you establish yourself. Once at the top, remember to give a helping hand to those who are below.

Some people cannot be helped. If a person you love is stuck in a state of denial regarding their own suffering or addictions, then there is a strong possibility that what you say or do will not make much of a difference. Do not fall into the trap of taking on someone else's burden as your own. It is too high of a price to pay. You will waste much valuable time, and your mental health will suffer. Half of your mastery of power comes from what you do not allow yourself to get dragged into. Neither the lazy nor the procrastinator can be helped. The best plans in the world will not do a thing for you, if you are unwilling to take action. One cannot motivate unmotivated people; inspiration must come from within. Do not waste your advice on the stubborn; they will never take it. Some people always look for others to blame, no matter how conspicuous their errors are. They are always the victim. How can you help someone who thinks that every failure in their life is someone else's fault? Soon enough, they will blame you. Some people always see a half-empty glass. Rather than seeing the positives, they cannot help but focus on the negatives. When they meet new people, they look out for anything and everything that may be wrong with them and, as a result, they are always waging wars with people and are constantly having unhealthy relationships. Some people are simply unintelligent and are just not amenable to reason. Some are born parasites—they only take and will never give anything back. Some are helplessly volatile—they have turbulent pasts, unstable careers, and a long line of broken relationships. Unless you are their psychiatrist, stay clear of them. They will drown you in their misfortune. Never give unsolicited advice. Learn to recognize those who cannot be helped. Do not waste your time or resources on them.

When in doubt, associate with the thoughtful and the prudent, those who know how to control their impulses, set goals, and follow plans. Sooner or later, they will have the upper hand. Avoid friends and lovers who live with a taste for champagne on a beer budget. Anyone who is obsessed with expensive things will find a way to get them, including draining their resources—and yours, if you are unfortunate enough to be in their lives. They are irredeemable. To them, as to Oscar Wilde, "anyone who lives within their means suffers from lack of imagination." What they really crave is attention. They would go broke to acquire an item that attracts attention to itself for the luxury it implies, whether it is a designer handbag or a glitzy mansion. While they spend money in a way that suggests that they have a lot of it, many are, in fact, poor or end up in poverty. Eccentricity is a hallmark of both creative genius and mental illness. In the rare instances where it is coupled with intellectual giftedness or extraordinary talent, it is the source of fame and fortune. In the absence of talent or wealth—which is the most common case—it will lead straight to infamy. Fame, whether positive or negative, always deals with extremes—geniuses or criminals, acclaim or castigation.

Whether looking for employees or business partners, choose people with both talent and principle. Intelligence is the number one predictor of work performance. It is at the root of both problem-solving ability and innovation. A strong work ethic can sometimes compensate where intelligence runs thin. If you are a manager, all it takes to separate the wheat from the chaff is to give your subordinates a tough assignment. Those who are truly talented and take both their job and their reputation seriously will not miss the opportunity to prove themselves. It is an effective way to gauge your subordinates' competence level and drive. Those whom nature truly made superior—not just in intelligence, but also in character—make the best partners. They are not just technically gifted, but are also conscientious people who take responsibility for their actions, are dependable, arrive on time, do what they say, and do not let the others in their team down. Untrustworthy and unreliable people will drain both your energy and resources. Competence alone is not enough. Integrity and drive are also needed.

Build relationships with those who are informed well, but not those who deal in vulgar gossip. It helps to be knowledgeable about current affairs. Some people are well-connected and well-liked. They have access to a great deal of useful information that may stay hidden to others. They are great colleagues or neighbors to know and befriend. Access to timely or restricted information is a great source of power, not to mention the new connections you may be able to make. Avoid those who speak ill of others behind their backs and spread gossip. Sooner or later, they will speak ill of you. They are dangerous and can do much harm if you confide in them. Gossip is always about lifting ourselves up by pushing others down. By its very nature, gossip is adversarial. It pits the gossiper against the person being talked about and asks the listener to pick a side. The purpose of gossip is to tear a person down and erode their self-esteem. Those who spread gossip are insecure, malicious, and untrustworthy. To avoid partaking in their vulgarity or being its target, avoid them altogether.

Surround yourself with people who are smarter than you. Check your ego at the door and realize that you are not always the smartest person in the room. Being surrounded by smarter people will not only challenge you to perform at your best, but it will also allow you to learn new things, gain new perspectives, and develop new ideas. The truly intelligent are highly flexible and able to thrive in different settings, they think before they speak or act, and are able to effectively manage their emotions. They know their limits and can admit it. They are also observant enough to see your own limits and make you realize them in tactful ways. Gravitate toward people who can offer alternative perspectives and make you realize when you are going in the wrong direction and need to change course. Seek out those who not only know more, but are willing to challenge and push you. Build relationships with those who can share their wins and positive vibes and help you realize that you can do the same. The right circle of influence raises the bar, helping us to set new, loftier expectations of ourselves. Oftentimes, we do not know what we are capable of until we see others achieve. Highly successful people are generally willing to share what it takes to make things happen. It may be important to learn from your own mistakes, but given how short life is, is it not even better to surround yourself with smart people in order to leverage what they have learnt from their mistakes on their journey to success?

11

Rule Five: Master Yourself

Knowing how to delay immediate pleasure in an effort to serve a more important and more gratifying goal makes all the difference in achieving that goal. The ability to effectively delay gratification is a sign of maturity. Indeed, children under five years of age demonstrate a marked lack of delayed gratification ability and most commonly seek immediate gratification. As the human prefrontal cortex develops and matures to become more complicated and connected with its pleasure and reward centers, older children and adults find deferment-of-gratification tasks easier than do young children. So behave like the adult that you are. Sometimes, immediate discomfort is the more beneficial choice. For the college student, it may mean foregoing tonight's party to study for the upcoming exam. For the budding entrepreneur, it may require long workdays, foregone vacations, and little pay for many years for greater professional independence and higher financial rewards down the road. Whether it is saving for your dream house or your retirement, choosing a healthy lifestyle now to stay healthy as you age, or putting up with a difficult job to help boost your career for the long run, delayed gratification can yield tremendous returns while helping you develop patience and self-control. Choosing to have something now might feel good, but making the effort to have discipline and manage your impulses can result in bigger rewards in the future. The ability to delay gratification is found to translate into better academic success, better physical and psychological health, higher social competence, and higher socioeconomic status. Maturity demands self-control, decorum, and composure. Always behave as though others were watching. It may make the difference between career advancement and career stagnation.

Learn to control your emotions. If your mind is overloaded with information, too many priorities, and no time to debate, it is likely that the emotional brain will overrule the rational one. Emotional decision-making is very fast in comparison to a rational decision and can be quite useful when faced with immediate danger or in decisions of minimal significance. Valuable decisions, however, deserve thoughtful analysis. People often make quick emotional decisions without knowing why, and then create post hoc, rational reasons to justify their poor emotional decisions. In high-stakes situations that involve competition and risk, it pays to take the slow road of rational decision-making. This can make all the difference between success and failure. Sometimes, immediate and unrelated emotions can create mistakes by distorting and creating bias in judgments, which can lead to reckless action. Controlling your emotions starts with becoming aware of them. Learn to attribute the source of your mood and assess whether or not it is related to the decision at hand. If you are feeling intensely emotional, consider delaying your response or choice until you feel calmer. In the meantime, focus on small activities that are emotionally neutral. Reframe the situation in more rational ways. Perhaps seek the counsel of a neutral party. Sometimes, all that is needed is a second pair of eyes.

The power of raw emotions can be overwhelming. Oftentimes, these emotions drive us to do things that we later regret. Anger is one such emotion. Lashing out may alleviate the feeling temporarily, but it does nothing to address the underlying issue, not to mention causing a few additional issues. Strong negative emotions—such as intense fear, sadness, and anger—can weaken your ability to solve problems, handle challenges effectively, and get along with others. In more severe cases, they may spiral into anxiety, depression, or violence. Intense positive emotions, such as love and affection, can also be destructive. They can impair your judgement and blind you to the sometimes self-serving interest of those whom you least suspect of deception. Intense joy or excitement can lead to taking reckless risks due to overconfidence. Emotional intelligence starts with self-regulation. Think before acting. Allow yourself to feel all your emotions, but resist acting on them while you are upset. Maturity consists of learning to tolerate uncomfortable feelings without throwing a fit. It reflects the ability to face emotional, social, and cognitive threats with patience and thoughtfulness. It is not the hand you are dealt, but how you react to it that matters most. Learn to view challenges as opportunities. Calm yourself down when upset. Cheer yourself up when feeling down. Temper your imagination when feeling overly excited. Be flexible. Put forth an effort and persevere in difficult times. See the good in others, but not so much as to be gullible. Set yourself achievable goals. Strive to find a creative way out when you hit a wall. Think or ask for help. When dealing with highly challenging goals, forget the outcome, keep your focus on the task at hand, and enjoy the process.

You cannot master yourself if you do not understand yourself. The best ways to know yourself—your intellect, temperament, abilities, and disabilities—are competition, trial and error, self-reflection, and other people's perceptions. All human characteristics are relative. It is all about knowing where we stand with respect to a measured average. The only way to know that we are gifted in mathematics is to demonstrate greater ease at solving complex mathematical problems compared to most other people, especially those who have proven themselves beforehand. We all have weaknesses that we are blind to or that simply were never revealed for lack of opportunity. They are exposed one day when we try our hand at something new, compete with others at a higher level, or pay heed to the words of those who are quick to notice defects in others. Much research indicates that our nearest and dearest often see us better than we see ourselves. Because it is so difficult to observe ourselves, we must rely on the observations of others, especially those who know us well. It is hard to know our true character unless others let us know how we affect them. One negative slant may simply reflect malicious intent, but you should take serious notice when viewpoints converge, especially if they come from generally respectable folks. Rather than feeling offended, take it as advice for self-improvement. And where improvement is not possible, you can at least use the information to your advantage by avoiding enterprises that rely on strength where you lack it.

Act boldly, but prudently. As Niccolò Machiavelli put it, "all courses of action are risky, so prudence is not in avoiding danger (it is impossible), but in calculating risk and acting decisively. Make mistakes of ambition and not mistakes of sloth. Develop the strength to do bold things, not the strength to suffer." The challenge is to be bold, but not to be bold and foolish. Some risks should not be taken because the consequences could be disastrous. With a good dose of discernment, however, we can take calculated risks that will benefit us regardless of the outcome. Consider the pros and cons of acting on a bold strategy. Think through how you might mitigate the risks. Give appropriate weight to what is to be gained and what could be lost. Do not be rash and commit yourself to a situation with little gain and much danger to yourself or others. Sometimes there is more courage in avoiding danger than in conquering it. Be diligent and cautious in sizing up the situation. Take your time. Once convinced of the path to take, act boldly and decisively. Some of life's most rewarding experiences—from starting your own business to finding your next lover—come as a result of taking risks. No action means accepting the status quo. Taking a risk to achieve a goal requires the courage to face the fear of uncertainty. By taking action you can build confidence. No matter the outcome—rejection, failure, change, loss, or gain—you will grow through the process and become more resilient and confident as a result of it.

Do not be hopelessly stubborn. Used with discernment, stubbornness can be a strong leadership quality and a key determinant of success. Sometimes great ideas are brought to life through sheer stubbornness. Being stubborn can make us persevere. It helps us stand our ground when everyone else is trying to tell us that we are wrong. Arguably, certain qualities, such as vision, focus, determination, and grit, are derivatives of stubbornness. Because stubborn people know what they want, they tend to be more decisive and get things done. But without reflection, stubbornness is nothing more than plain stupidity. The pathway to greatness is the ability to admit fault when a wrong decision has been made. It makes no sense to stay the course when there is overwhelming evidence that you are wrong. Check your pride at the door and listen to what others are trying to tell you. They may have a valid point. The first step may be to understand what drives your compulsion to be right at all costs. Let go of your rigidity and close-mindedness. Even when you are right, it can be good to make concessions—people will recognize that you were right, but admire your courtesy. Learn to appreciate the value of looking at issues from different perspectives. When you are weaker, never fight for honor's sake; choose surrender instead. It is the smart thing to do—surrendering will give you time to recover and adjust. Being overly competitive can blind us to the qualities of those we are competing against. If you end up losing, rather than taking it out on the opposition, try to learn from your mistakes. Good sportsmanship demands the ability to remain respectful and recognize our adversary's strengths. Do not defend the wrong side out of pride and stubbornness, just because your opponent happened to choose the best option first. Being able to acknowledge that others can be more discerning at times demonstrates strength of character and maturity.

Prudence consists of the golden middle way, the sweet spot between two extremes, one of excess and the other of deficiency. According to Aristotle, courage taken to excess is recklessness and, in deficiency, cowardice. Push right-wing politics too far and you will end up with fascism. Push too far to the left and you will find yourself in anarchy. In all things, exercise common sense, self-restraint, and moderation. Speak prudently. Keep it short and sweet. The more you say, the more you open yourself up for criticism. Do not speak ill of your adversaries. Temper your opinions. A good lawyer knows that there are valid arguments to be made both ways on any issue. When the masses have sided with stupidity, bite your tongue. Because it disdains and condemns the judgement of others, dissent is often taken as an insult. It rarely helps to have the majority opinion against you. When in Rome, you might as well do as the Romans do. Temper your antipathy. Sometimes we dislike a person viscerally without knowing why. In our ancestral past, neighboring tribes are known to have often been hostile to each other. So evolution may have instilled in us an instinctive fear of people who are different from us, perhaps, because we unconsciously perceive threat in outsiders. Make the mindful choice of compassion, rather than aggression. Get to know the person first. You might find out that they are a truly accomplished individual. Make friends, rather than enemies, especially of those in positions of power. Open up to others, but not too much. Communication can reveal the defects that reservation had hidden. Choose dignity over excessive familiarity, for the latter breeds contempt. Have a sense of humor, but know to be serious when the circumstances warrant it. Avoid eccentricity—short of being a genius, you might be labeled odd or unstable. Temper your behavior. Do not give into every common impulse. Impulsivity is a hallmark of both mania and psychopathy. Choose the path of patience and reason. When in doubt, look things over twice. Being known for prudence is the ultimate kind of fame.

Do not be fickle. A mixture of moody and indecisive, fickle-minded people go whichever way the wind blows. You cannot depend on them because they may back out of a commitment at the last minute. You cannot confide in them because they are not capable of loyalty. They will promise everything and deliver nothing. They start something new frequently, but never actually finish anything. Perennially indecisive, they can never quite make up their minds. Their mercurial mood is always on the move. In fact, the only thing constant about them is their inconstancy. Nobody can depend on an unreliable person, including your coworkers, your spouse, your friends, and even your acquaintances. To retain their worth, words should be backed up by deeds. Keep alienating everyone around you and, soon enough, you will find yourself all alone and broken. Having a strong reputation for consistently doing what you say, delivering on your commitments, and keeping your promises will have a profoundly positive impact on how others rate you in both your personal and professional life. You will gain respect and make friends. Your relationships will improve. You may even get that job promotion you have been dreaming of.

When a close relationship ends up badly, do not take advantage of the trust that was once placed in you. It is hard enough to cope with the pain of a bad breakup. Further betrayal will only deepen the wounds. Friends whom you have offended make the bitterest of enemies. Developing a reputation for being a backstabber will rarely benefit you. Some people are wolves in sheep's clothing. They may not react immediately in the face of perceived treachery, but they will hit you back with twice the force when the opportunity permits it. Keep your desire for vengeance in check. Acknowledge your feelings, but know how to move beyond your anger, bitterness, and resentment. Simply putting some distance between you may be enough to open an ever-expanding rift, which may eventually bring a slow end to the relationship. Sometimes the most suitable strategy for dealing with troubles is to forget them.

Some people have egos made of glass. Even a loving tease may break them. Those who deal with them must walk on eggshells and never forget their delicacy. They need external validation and never have enough. They bend and contort all conversations and comments into some sort of threat or attack directly aimed at themselves. Deep down, they tend to be unhappy with themselves and with who they are. Negative feedback from external sources, even if constructive, never misses to find fertile ground in them for self-criticism and self-deprecation. With them, it is all about damage control, even when there are no signs that damage has been done. When someone's ego is that brittle, all that matters is self-defense, which generally takes the form of attacks on others. People with strong egos know how to handle negative feedback better because, rather than seeing it as a threat, they see it as information about themselves that they can evaluate, learn, and grow from, or even reject if necessary. They can laugh off caustic humor. They can view the bigger picture and make more accurate causal attributions than personal and persecutory ones. Not everyone is out to get you. Most people are too self-centered to care that much about you. So know your insecurities and work to resolve them, either alone or with the help of a therapist.

Resilience is a muscle that can be developed. We are all born with a threshold beyond which we may break down. But we all have a range of emotional resilience within which we can grow. Those who are the most successful are often also those who have failed the most. Do not allow the momentary pain to darken your outlook on life and make you abstain from new experiences. We fear failure, in part, because we fear that people who witness it will somehow think less of us. The truth is that most people are so preoccupied with their own lives that they hardly take notice of our failure or suffering. Besides, our sufferings are never as earth-shattering as we think they are. The world will move on and so will we. Winston Churchill said, "You will make all kinds of mistakes; but as long as you are generous and true and, also, fierce, you cannot hurt the world or even seriously distress her. She was made to be wooed and won by youth. She has lived and thrived only by repeated subjugations." Even the most painful of failures represent an opportunity to grow. You can learn from them and do things differently in the future. Acknowledge the pain, but learn to accept the events and plot a way forward. We only experience real, lasting failure when we let our setbacks knock us down for good.

Self-mastery will lead to reserve, a seal of true talent. Reserved people are naturally calmer and more collected. Nothing much can rile them up. They take their time with anything and will not rush into actions. They are good at maintaining a steady, stable mood. They do not like to create drama by airing their dirty laundry in public. Instead, they are quite self-sufficient, as they know how to effectively manage their feelings. As a result, they have a calming effect on those who are more high-strung. They enjoy socializing, but do not mind some quiet time alone. Because they are comfortable with themselves, they can spend hours thinking about things without realizing where the time has gone. This makes them both self-aware and thoughtful. By not reacting as rashly or irrationally as some other people tend to, they give themselves the opportunity to be very consistent. They look before they leap, which makes them good at setting long-term goals, planning for the unexpected, and avoiding unnecessary risks. Their propensity for deliberation gives them a greater advantage when it comes to critical thinking and problem-solving. They are good listeners and choose their words wisely when they speak up. They are highly observant people who can accurately read the room. As a result, they are more likely to notice people's body language and facial expressions, which makes them better at interpersonal communication. They do not get overly stressed by changes in circumstances because they are a bit more withdrawn from it all anyway. As they are not hugely affected by their surroundings or by other people's behavior, they tend to be easygoing and relaxed. They are also very reflective because they can step back and analyze what is going on, which helps them enjoy the moment more, rather than rushing through experiences or constantly chasing the next short-term pleasure. This helps them be more rounded and consistent in general. They know how to display their talent without coming across as flamboyant self-promoters. They shy away from expressing strong opinions and are versed in the art of diplomacy. They make loyal, attentive, and committed friends, who would rather have a few close, trusted friendships to invest their time and energy in, as opposed to a large network of acquaintances. The same qualities also make them great romantic or business partners. They make great leaders because they listen well and have great emotional empathy—skills useful for getting the most out of a team. The aura of mystery and intelligence they exude leaves others curious to know more about them. Strangers instinctively respect them without quite knowing why. Reserve—a child of the careful, sensitive temperament—can also be acquired and developed, just like resilience.

12

Rule Six: Leverage the Norm of Reciprocity

Place people into your debt by strategically doing them favors. When you invest in your relationships—whether professional or personal—you can reap benefits from them. The ancestral norm of reciprocity will make those you help out of difficulty feel indebted to you, which may lead them to do you an even greater favor at a future time. What is needed to set the halo effect in motion can be as simple as taking the time to listen to a colleague in distress and uttering a few comforting words of kindness. Their gratitude will lead to favors and a whole host of positive attributions, including superior character, talent, and even merit. Success can sometimes be purchased with affection. Merit can take a shortcut when helped by favor. Strategically granting favors does not mean, however, turning into a people pleaser—someone, who out of a severe deficiency in self-esteem, will consistently put the needs of others before their own in a desperate effort to be liked. People can smell weakness, and those with a penchant for exploiting others will not miss an opportunity to take advantage of your benevolence as much as they can. This is the surest way to develop resentment, passive-aggression, stress, depression, insomnia, and more. Beware the psychopaths. They are born parasites and, quite literally, lack the brain areas needed for empathy. Either learn to recognize them at a glance or, at the very least, blacklist them when they fail to honor the norm of reciprocity. Unless you specifically intend to be charitable, do not waste your favors on those who can never pay you back. The less costly your favors, the better. Reputation can be purchased with kind words. Simply remembering someone's birthday or congratulating them upon a promotion can win tremendous goodwill. Courtesy is the cheapest way that successful people win the good graces of others.

"If you would be loved, love and be lovable," said Benjamin Franklin. Human relationships are all about giving and taking—you get what you give. When you are in a leadership position, be known for pleasing others. When a person of authority is genuine, he or she will naturally attract like minds. Respectfully sincere, frank, and forthright behavior has a habit of spreading, especially when it comes from the top. Machiavelli said that it was best for a leader to be both feared and loved. But since this is almost impossible to achieve, he proposed that a leader is better off being feared than loved. Fear breeds resentment and distrust, however, not respect. When good deeds are not acknowledged and when bad deeds are always brought to the fore, cynicism finds fertile ground to flourish. And what consequences does fear bring when the going gets tough? Will your team members be in the trenches with you? Or will they simply get up and leave? Your associates will thrive when they feel valued, and you will gain their respect and affection. If you stand up for them, they will stand up for you when adversity strikes. Earning the respect of the team means being open, fair, willing to listen, to admit error, share in the difficulty, and act to protect the team's well-being. But earning respect also means enforcing the team's core values, organizational policies, and insisting on peak performance and work ethic. The key is to strike a balance: being compassionate without coming across as weak, being understanding without letting anyone cross a line they should not, and managing emotions without losing sight of objectives.

Build a circle of trusted friends in prosperity and health, just like you build your nest egg in youth. Your generosity will win you friends, adversity will prove them. Keep a following of grateful people—someday, they may return your favors. When you give other people gifts, there is a good chance that you will get gifts as well. Gifting promotes social bonding and cooperation.

Nobody is so fortunate as to never face hardship. Close friends can be key to building resilience in challenging circumstances. When the going gets tough, your best friends can facilitate effective ways of coping, including planning, reframing an issue in a positive way, and providing emotional support. Nobody is so perfect as to never need advice. Even world leaders surround themselves with whole cabinets of advisers. A good friend's experience can spare you the cost of a learning curve. Always leave the door open for friendship—help may come through it.

Make good use of the favors people owe you. Reciprocity and cooperation are the underpinnings of a civilized society—they allow us to help people who need it and hope that they will help us when we need it. The desire to repay goodwill is hardwired in the human brain. Make judicious use of it. Keep the favors owed by your powerful friends for greater occasions. Do not waste them on matters of little importance. Do not trade a bigger favor for a trivial one. A long-forgotten gesture of goodwill may get you nothing. Its memory may be short-lived. Tactfully bring it back to life. Keep the exchanges going. Deeds can be bought with kind words. Most human decisions are emotional. Warm feelings will trigger compassionate deeds. Ask for favors infrequently. Asking for too much, too often will make you look weak and needy and turn off others. And never forget to express your gratitude no matter how small the favor received.

Be tactful when you ask for a favor. Timing is of the essence. People will grant your wishes more readily if they are in good spirits. They may think that you are selfish and incapable of empathy if you burden them with your request for a favor in the midst of a raging tempest. Humans have an unconscious tendency of attributing moods to unrelated events. You want no thread between someone's foul mood and your request. If you catch them in a bad mood, forget about asking for anything. Simply help them get into a good mood. This can have the same effect as doing them a favor, which should leave them feeling indebted. Ask them later, when you catch them in better spirits. When you see someone else being refused something, run the other way. The fear of saying *no* is all but gone. Doing someone a favor beforehand is always excellent currency. Do not ask in an intimidating manner or try to pressure anyone into doing something. Let their conscience be free when they choose to say *no*. Someone can genuinely have other pressing demands. They should not be made to feel bad for wanting to delay repaying your debt, especially when they have a reputation for being generally honorable.

Find each person's insecurities, their weak points, and provide them the reassurance they need. You can potentially trade this low-cost favor for a high-cost favor down the road. The key to moving other people's will is to grant them what they want and tell them what they need to hear. This may include tapping into their fantasies. According to Robert Greene, "life is so harsh and distressing that people who can manufacture romance or conjure up fantasy are like oases in the desert. Every one flocks to them." Finding someone's handle requires social skill in sizing up their character. Whilst some of this skill stems from inborn ability, a decent part of it can be acquired. Just like for any other skill, practice makes perfect. The best way to improve your social skills is to be social. As Sigmund Freud remarked, "no mortal can keep a secret. If his lips are silent, he chatters with his fingertips; betrayal oozes out of him at every pore." Pay attention to the person's seemingly unimportant gestures, facial expressions, and passing words. You can also share a minor secret with them. Appearing vulnerable will fracture their armor and open up trust—they may reveal a much bigger secret in return. Look for the dissatisfied, the unhappy, and the insecure. Such people are riddled with weaknesses and have needs that you can fill. Look for passions and obsessions that cannot be controlled. The stronger the passion, the more vulnerable the person. And what people cannot control, you can control for them.

Noticing merit early and rewarding it at the germinal stage can pass for a favor. This skill is especially useful to managers. By bestowing your subordinates' well-deserved reward early, you can make them feel indebted to you and earn their gratitude and loyalty. This is a subtle trick, whereby all you are really doing is paying a debt, but you are making it pass for a favor, which creates an obligation for the receiver. It is a low-cost way to purchase referent power and earn the goodwill of those you are managing. It requires sublime judgement, which is an ability that certain people are born with.

They perfect it with age and experience. Others cannot help but recognize their secret strength and innate authority. When also blessed with technical skill, ambition, resilience, and perseverance, they are those who are truly born to lead.

Grant someone a concession to get what you want. It is a well-known and well-utilized tactic by savvy salespeople everywhere. You start by asking for too much, and then strategically lower your demand. If you are in the business of selling suits, for instance, you may present the customer with your most exquisite and highest priced suit first. The person will most likely reject the offer. This will make them feel bad for turning down your first request, making them more likely to say *yes* to your second smaller or lower-cost request, which is what you really wanted in the first place. Making strategic concessions at the right time can also be an effective tactic to obtain compliance during more complex, high-stakes negotiations. Coming prepared to manage the rapidly changing dynamics of such negotiations is paramount to success. Make sure you know the positions, goals, and interests of each party and prepare a list of concessions you are willing to make. Be slow to yield a concession and make sure that your counterpart clearly understands and appreciates the particular concession's cost and value to you. Understanding the full scale of your sacrifice should affect the other party's perception of your goodwill and increase their trust and desire to reciprocate. To increase the likelihood that you get something in return for your concession, try to explicitly—but tactfully—demand reciprocity. As the negotiation moves forward, initial concessions are replaced with increasingly smaller ones, and the participants work towards finding a mutually acceptable point between each of their opening positions. Effective negotiators aim to achieve a mutually acceptable result that satisfies the interests of both sides at the lowest cost to each, resulting in a win-win situation. When the other party is too self-interested to care about reciprocating your goodwill, make your concession contingent upon a specified concession of equal value in return. Learn to recognize untrustworthy people in any exchange situation. If your counterpart is showing flagrant disrespect for anything you propose, the most powerful thing you can do is to walk away from the negotiation at once.

The French philosopher Jean de La Bruyère wrote, "The shortest and best way to make your fortune is to let people see clearly that it is in their interests to promote yours." As humans, we have the tendency to act for the sake of promoting our own best interests. Everything we do, we do it because, at some level (whether consciously or unconsciously), we believe that doing so will benefit us in some way. Even acts of virtue, which appear to be selfless, are intrinsically mercenary and driven by self-interest, like the pursuit of a life of morality in the hope that the resulting reputation will be convertible—through reciprocation, increased opportunities for exchange, or the force of authority—into abundant benefits and riches. Know that others are primarily interested in themselves and in what matters to them. If you are asking others to commit themselves or their resources to your cause, it is natural that they may want to know what they have to gain personally from it. Like a good negotiator, formulate your request as a win-win proposition, whereby the other party clearly understands that by helping you, they will, in some way, help themselves. A good elevator pitch or sales presentation should always emphasize the benefits that a prospect can expect from a product or service. If you want to captivate the attention of your audience while giving a public speech, be sure to tell them why they should be spending the next hour listening to you, rather than attending to some other business. Many start-ups will grant employees stock options to give them a stake in the success of the business. When asking for help, make sure to appeal to people's self-interest, never to their mercy or gratitude. Give them a stake. Show them what they stand to gain, and they may help you get what you want.

To make someone like you more, use the Benjamin Franklin effect, a cognitive bias which causes people to like someone more after they do that person a favor, especially if they previously disliked that person or felt neutral toward them. In his autobiography, Benjamin Franklin, a scientist and politician, proposed that "he that has once done you a kindness will be more ready to do you another, than he whom you yourself have obliged." The concept is based on the way that Franklin dealt with the animosity of a rival legislator. Specifically, after hearing that his rival had a rare book in his library, Franklin wrote to him and asked whether he could borrow the book for a few days. The rival agreed and, a week later, Franklin returned the book with a letter expressing how much he liked it. The next time that the two met, Franklin's rival spoke to him with great civility and showed a willingness to help him in other matters, leading the two men to become good friends. What happens when someone does you a favor is that they need to be able to justify it to themself, in order to avoid the cognitive dissonance that would occur from doing something positive for someone that they dislike. The simplest way to do this is generally to convince themselves that they must like you enough to do you that favor, even if that was not originally the case. This, in turn, may lead them to actually like you and do you other favors in the future. Franklin's subtle skill consists of foreseeing an insult and cleverly turning it into gratitude.

Gifting is an art that needs to be done just the right way. The most appreciated gifts are those that cost little, but are much desired. For instance, you can do other people valuable favors that take no more than five minutes, such as making an introduction, giving feedback, and offering advice. The discomfort of not being able to return a costly favor may cause an otherwise grateful person to break off their relationship with you entirely. Gifting from a manager to a subordinate should always be done with the utmost care so as not to be perceived as quid pro quo or even harassment. Performing a favor for someone whose status is far above your own could be viewed cynically by the recipient. They are likely to read selfish intentions into it, given that some people do favors for the powerful in order to get themselves a leg up. You stand a better chance at gaining their trust by simply being kind, rather than doing a kind deed. A thoughtful gift of token value is oftentimes a great way to show your appreciation to anyone. Courtesy is the best of all gifts. It costs little and powerfully binds others.

13

Rule Seven: Develop Social Tact

Power is a social game. It takes skill to play it the right way. Bulldogs and sharks can have their moments of glory, but they cannot help but make enemies. Enemies, in turn, can make their lives miserable by resisting, sabotaging, or downright attacking them. Do not make yourself disliked, whether in your personal or professional life. If you want others to recognize and reward your accomplishments, recognize and reward theirs. Give them the credit they deserve. Make them look good in front of the people who are important to them. Be sincerely nice to everyone, not just the people who you think can help you. People can sense phoniness—and everyone resents it. Swallow the impulse to offend, even if the other person seems weak. You never know where each of you may end up in the future or which way your paths may cross again. People may not remember what you said exactly, but they will remember how you made them feel. Companies know that customers are far more likely to share bad experiences than good ones with others. It is no different in interpersonal relationships. Remember that what you say or do has an impact on others, sometimes in a deeply emotional way. Try as best as you can to use words and actions that result in positive experiences and emotions for the people you are interacting with.

Mind your manners. When in doubt, err on the side of being gracious. The only way to be loved is to be courteous and pleasant. Take notice of the bad behavior of others, not to imitate it, but to defend yourself from it.

Those who are skilled at human interactions know to adapt themselves to the temperament and intelligence of others. Avoid being sarcastic or putting other people down. The fleeting feeling of satisfaction is not worth the long-run costs. Given the importance people put on intelligence, never impugn on another person's mental abilities. Understand other people's character in order to please them the right way and be mindful of their feelings. Always remember to return favors done to you. Only speak of another person publicly in order to praise them, never to point out their faults. Highlighting someone else's defects will neither hide yours nor console you from having them. One can find something praiseworthy to say to just about anyone. The secret lies in focusing on the good, rather than the bad. Understand that it is hard to always do things well and that everyone is prone to making mistakes. Give others the benefit of the doubt and be quick to forgive. Consider it an honor to be criticized, especially by those who speak ill of good people. Only truly high-status people can afford magnanimity. So be the rare person to speak well of your enemy. Words can have enormous purchasing power. The right words delivered with the right tone and in the right manner can get you out of an impossible situation. Master the subtle art of selling air. Choose gentle words and deliver them even more gently.

Do your best to avoid schadenfreude—that instinctive twinge of excitement that we sometimes feel at someone else's pain or failure. When it comes along, try to think about why you are feeling that way instead of ignoring it out of guilt or self-disgust. Did you think the person deserved comeuppance and why? Do you envy the person whose misfortune you are enjoying? Were they making you feel inadequate or inferior? Did they betray you in the past? Perhaps you see them as an opponent. Perhaps it offers you consolation to know that you are not alone in your disappointments, but are part of a community of the failed. Schadenfreude is one of those mental traps that we fall into when we spend too much time comparing ourselves to others. The desire to have a competitive edge over another human being has evolutionary roots, and observing another individual's misfortune can induce joy, as it validates the observer's personal identity and boosts their self-esteem. Indulge with moderation. Schadenfreude is not the healthiest coping strategy available. In the future, when you recognize the emotion of schadenfreude in you, focus on what you could be doing with your time to better your life and your self. Strengthen your capacity for empathy. Put yourself in the other person's shoes and do your best to show some concern and sympathy instead.

Do not become known for always whining and complaining. Complaints will bring you discredit. Anybody can complain about a problem. The truly intelligent and capable people are those who prevent or solve problems. Develop a reputation for being a problem-solver instead. Become great at what you do by building up your expertise and competence. Show up early, do your work diligently, and leave late. Do not publicize slights, only how helpful others have been. Berating others will only earn you enemies. Learn to forgive. Nothing is more praiseworthy than speaking well of those who speak ill of you. One can go wrong inadvertently while having good intentions. Blasting another person with anger is like throwing hot coals with bare hands: both people get burned. Pause, even for a short while. If you still feel wronged after giving yourself time to process your emotions, calm down, and see the bigger picture, then shrink the relationship to a size that is safe. In the garden of your life, you may have to pull some weeds, but you should mainly focus on planting flowers.

Machiavelli wrote, "Any man who tries to be good all the time is bound to come to ruin among the great many who are not good." Being good-natured does mean being naive or weak. People often hide their motives. Deception is common. There are folks who can craftily wrap you into a web of guilt and a false sense of responsibility to them in order to snare you into a burdensome relationship that does nothing but benefit themselves. Manipulative people have a mission, and you are only a tool for their accomplishments. Learn to decipher hidden agendas. Having good theory of mind is a big component of social intelligence. The skill is partly genetic and partly acquired. Do not become impressed by anyone at first glance. Some people are but an empty shell with an ornate facade. What seems too good to be true usually disappoints. Conversely, seemingly catastrophic events often have a silver lining. Suspend your judgment and give yourself time to probe deeper than the surface. Pause before answering someone who contradicts you. Some people will feign disbelief to extract secrets from others, which they will then use against them. Those to whom lying comes easily are especially keen to throw dust into other people's eyes. They will promise everything and deliver nothing. Excessive courtesy is flattery—do not be fooled by it. As human beings, we are attuned fairly well to elusiveness in a person. When an encounter leaves you feeling poorly about the interaction, trust your instinct and beware accordingly. Cut toxic people out of your life sooner rather than later. In the long run, it will spare you grief, heartache, and much more.

Learn the art of indirection. Should you get a hostile question or a snide remark—be it while giving a public presentation, attending a work meeting, or at a social gathering—do your best to remain calm and in control. The attack often comes in the form of an innuendo, an indirect remark with the intent to disparage that works obliquely by way of allusion. These thinly veiled challenges to your credibility, knowledge, or integrity can easily make you lose your train of thought and leave you sweating in place. Learn to catch the poisonous darts as skillfully as they are hurled by the malicious individual. Do not take the bait and become defensive. Refrain from becoming hostile yourself. Sometimes an elegant joke will suffice to diffuse the tension and redirect the conversation. You can also look away from the hostile person and rephrase the question or remark with more neutral words while focusing your gaze on the other members of the gathering or audience. Your listeners will be impressed with you if you can, artfully and eloquently, sidestep the question being asked by answering a related, but more neutral, question instead. If you do that with enough confidence and conviction, even the questioner is likely to forget exactly what he or she originally asked. Some insinuations have good intent behind them and are used to probe other people's inclinations with regard to a delicate matter, out of an abundance of precaution, or to save face. For instance, a cleverly worded insinuation can convey sexual interest and indirectly probe the heart of another. An allusion can lessen the impact of delivering bad news. One can use a euphemism to address a subject that might be deemed negative or embarrassing. The key is to skillfully code or decode intent: the indirection may be created for innocent, well-intentioned purposes, or nefariously and cynically to purposefully deceive and confuse. Mastering the art of insinuation and good rhetoric are skills that any of us can benefit from, not just those who are in public roles.

Get over your fear of talking to people who are in a position of authority. Whether you are a student or an entry-level employee, talking to your professor, supervisor, or boss can be intimidating. One fears being judged the wrong way. Imagination rushes ahead and makes those in a position of authority seem much more than they truly are. Remember that, besides hard work and ability, luck also plays a big part in obtaining rank. Many people seem great until you mingle with them, and communication leads more often to disappointment than to esteem. Instead of putting them on a pedestal, try to see the person behind the title. They, too, want to impress you and look competent. Also remember that it is in the job description of your professors and work supervisors to talk with students and employees. They are there to listen to your concerns, questions, and just about everything related to your class or job. Many of them truly enjoy those discussions. It makes them feel recognized and appreciated for what they do. Coming prepared for the discussion ahead of time will help boost your confidence and allow you to keep it brief but to the point. Stand up straight, make direct eye contact, and speak in a normal voice. If you are meeting them for the first time, make sure your handshake is firm. Listen attentively and nod. You want them to find you likable, but also worthy of respect.

A dose of wit is good seasoning. Not everything should be taken seriously. One can find clever humor even in the most sobering situations. Mark Twain said that, "Humor is the great thing, the saving thing after all. The minute it crops up, all our hardnesses yield, all our irritations and resentments flit away, and a sunny spirit takes their place." Humor can do wonders for our health: reframing a negative event in a humorous light can act as an emotional filter, preventing the negativity from triggering a depressive episode. Laughter can also improve immune system function and cardiovascular health by diffusing anxiety and worry. The benefits go even further to confer better self-esteem, more positive affect, greater self-competency, and better performance in social interactions. Humor is, however, a tool that requires artful use. While jokes generally function as well-intended social glue, they may have the opposite effect if they are perceived as thinly veiled brags or as insulting to specific people or ideas. Sarcasm, for instance, involves saying one thing and meaning the opposite, which means that there is a risk of misunderstanding or worse if the recipient does not pick up on the humorous intent and takes a sarcastic comment literally. Only use sarcasm with familiar people with whom trust has been established and to whom the good intent is clear, but tone it down with new colleagues, in unfamiliar settings, or in a group where strong relationships have not yet been built. While self-deprecating humor can be an effective method of neutralizing negative information about oneself, among lower-status people it can backfire if the trait or skill in question is an essential area of competence. When humor is skillfully used to dodge difficult questions, it can cast the speaker in a positive light by highlighting his or her mental acuity. Learn to appreciate other people's humor and know how to take a joke. Delight in the absurdity of life and in the jokes you hear. While having a good sense of humor has genetic components, it can also be nurtured and developed. A good way to start is to practice looking at the funny side of life.

As you climb up the social ladder, take great care not to become unapproachable. For a manager, being approachable is a precondition of trust and open communication with your subordinates. It means being easy to deal with and easy to understand and connect with. It means showing respect for others' opinions, even if contrary to yours or out of the mainstream of thought. It means that your teammates are able to bring issues to you before they become full-blown crises because they know that you will not react badly. It is key to creating a strong team in which trust, confidence, and ideas can flow. So avoid being judgmental. Do not shoot people down. Be accessible and relatable. Walk the talk. Be sincere and genuine. Be a good listener. Your subordinates are paying close attention to your words, body language, facial expression, and reactions to get a read on you. Strive to maintain a friendly, open, and calm demeanor in all situations. Say what you mean verbally and nonverbally, and others will feel closer to you and more confident in trusting you.

Avoid flaunting your wealth and good fortune. It is a recipe for resentment. People will start finding faults where there are none out of simple envy. And if the government does not get you, regular citizens will. The common attitude among those who feel left behind will be to attribute your wealth to acts of dishonesty, rather than actual accomplishments. Being the target of class warfare is no fun. Understand that good luck plays a big part in extreme success, besides inborn ability and hard work. When you realize that despite all your hard work, you are probably luckier than most, you will lessen the chance of coming across as an arrogant snob and can better assimilate among ordinary people. Those who are the most insecure and the most desperate for attention are also those who flash their designer bags and luxury cars most ostentatiously. It is best not to be associated with the vain and the shallow. By being low-key, you will come across as a person of substance. You might be brilliant, but brilliant people are intimidating. Sometimes, it pays to look dumber than your mark. You may have a tremendous amount of success, but do not forget to be genuinely happy for others and to never belittle their achievements. There should be enough praise to go around for everyone. The self-made remember how many times they failed before succeeding. Mention some of your failures or venial faults. It will make you look both more unassuming and more relatable. When you are powerful or wealthy, you are never quite sure whether a person showing interest in you likes you for who you are or for the benefits they think you may provide to them. Practicing "stealth wealth" will make it more likely that you will have genuine relationships that do not bear the taint of money. Extreme success is, however, hard to fully hide. So be sure to show your generosity. Society rarely pardons those who are unwilling to give something back.

Not all situations demand the same level of openness and not all truths should be spoken. Do not volunteer explanations when nobody is asking for them. Silence is always an option. To offer excuses before they are called for is to incriminate yourself. Lying to promote one's self-interests at the expense of others or to simply inflict harm on others fully deserves its bad reputation. But lying can have a prosocial motive. When we tell our significant other that he or she looks great before a date to boost his or her self-esteem, we lie precisely because we care about our partner. A bitter pill is best delivered in sugarcoating. By rephrasing a bad performance review to a low-performing employee as constructive criticism, you will be delivering the bad news along with the remedy, thus lessening the pain. In distant relationships, telling the brutal truth can damage the relationship and reduce trust. It may be best to let someone else be the bearer of bad news. Sometimes it is enough to allude to things to get the message across. In competitive situations, those who show all their cards risk losing. Anyone in business should master the art of dissimulation. When hungry enough, dogs will eat dogs. A successful salesperson knows to always keep his or her prospecting tricks secret. If you keep your intensions to yourself and make it a purpose to never reveal the aim behind your actions, you deny others the opportunity to stop, copy, criticize, or flatter you. If they have no clue what you are up to, your adversaries cannot possibly prepare a defense either. You can make them lose their sense of control if you lead them far enough down the wrong path. Your unpredictability and seeming lack of consistency will keep them off-kilter, and they will wear themselves thin trying to understand your moves. Fibbing may be your best option when someone is asking for your opinion and you just do not have anything nice to say. Telling a white lie or withholding the truth may make the difference between keeping the peace and making an enemy. If you make yourself vulnerable to a toxic person by sharing your true self, it is possible that they will use it against you in some way. The best policy may be to keep such people at arm's length. Not everyone is entitled to know your life story or have access to your authentic self. If telling the whole truth will make you unsafe, ruin your reputation, or bring you trouble, opt for a white lie when keeping quiet is not a possibility.

No matter how close you are to someone, the laws of politeness should prevail. Do not stand on ceremony, but do not become complacent in your manners or courtesy either. Always be sure to keep a safe distance with respect to others. Deal with them in a grand way. Too much affection will diminish esteem. Remain mysterious by never revealing yourself completely. Anything arcane causes veneration. Do not pay too much heed to whatever may be going on in their lives either. Do not comment on the ills of others. A gossip is always detested. There is no need to share all of your secrets with your friends, even your blood relationships. Confidences are burdens. They turn whomever confided into a slave to the whims of their confidants. Should a friend's secret become known through no fault of yours, they may turn into your worst enemy, especially if they hold more power than you. We are all liable to do something foolish at some point in our lives. Unless you find yourself in a position of having to disclose the event, keep it to yourself. Those who commonly prey on other people's weaknesses will not miss an opportunity to strike where it hurts. Never doubt the power of a single moment's mistake to void a lifetime of good deeds. Avoid doing business with family or close friends. Family money is often said to be the easiest to get, but it can also be the most expensive. When the deal goes bad, your relationship will be irredeemably tainted—whether subtly or dramatically—by the experience. Unlike a stranger, the scornful family member is likely to remain in your life forever, constantly reminding you of the bad experience and possibly harming your other relationships. Family baggage can plague family businesses. Jealousy and resentment from childhood can cloud business judgment. Family members can be quick to see disagreements as disloyalty. A good friend does not always equal a good business partner, as he or she may have a very different work ethic from you. With good planning, communication, and luck, things could work out, but you would be better off staying away from landmines if you can.

Become a good conversationalist. If you avoid talking about yourself, you will neither be praising yourself nor revealing any weakness. Both can be cause for embarrassment. Everyone loves to talk about themselves, which is why a good listener—a scant presence at any venue—is always liked. Understand that others just cannot wait to get the microphone and tell you all about what they like doing and what they have achieved. And by not talking about yourself, you are giving them center stage, and they will love it without realizing it. A simple way to stop talking about yourself is to ask an open-ended question and let the other person speak. Be present and genuinely interested in what they are saying. Become a person of substance by reading and informing yourself on a variety of topics from world affairs to business and culture. You will be seeding the conversation with jolts instead of sounding like a broken record, repeating a story heard a thousand times. When asked a question, keep your answer short enough to retain interest, but long enough to cover the subject. Go for the positive topics and converse amiably. Do not argue. A conversation should be a platform where opinions are aired, not a battleground to pit one's stance against another. There is not always a common ground to every debate. Respect other people's opinions and allow for things to be left open-ended. And never forget courtesy. Just like any other skill, becoming a good conversationalist requires practice. So become more social and learn from those who have already mastered the art.

14

Rule Eight: Become Self-Reliant

Friedrich Nietzsche wrote, "It is the business of the very few to be independent; it is a privilege of the strong. And whoever attempts it, even with the best right, but without being obliged to do so, proves that he is probably not only strong, but also daring beyond measure." What Nietzsche meant is that there are very few people who are up to the task of venturing out into the unknown by themselves to ponder deep questions about the nature of the human soul. The unknowns of the human psyche set aside, those who have developed the ability to think independently are exceedingly rare, even among the best educated. Many possess a stunning ability to memorize—few are those who can penetrate deeper to unearth cause-and-effect relationships. Dogma is everywhere. Do not be trapped by it. It is incredibly important to ask yourself whose interest it stands to promote and whether those interests are consistent with your own sense of self. Life is short. You will not get a second shot at it. Do not waste your precious life by living it on someone else's terms. Independent thinking will enable you to become more discerning about the things you hear, see, and believe and help you question values and assumptions. It will also help you to better know yourself and what you want in life instead of living it according to other people's wishes and templates. We are all born alone and we will all die alone, so we each have to take responsibility for our lives at every step along the way. Become a cynic and develop the habit of instinctively distrusting thoughts that rely on conventional wisdom. Suspend judgement until you have confirmed that there is reality behind the logic. Know yourself so that you can become secure with who you are and what you believe in. Nothing is more empowering than knowing that you are in control of your own life and your own choices. Learn to think independently. Your happiness hinges on it.

Those who entrust their destiny into other people's hands are bound for a life of disappointment. In the self-centered and overwhelmed minds of others, you are but a fleeting afterthought. Some people are terrified at the sole thought of having to face life's challenges alone. So they opt for codependency, relying on someone else—usually a significant other, sometimes a family member or friend—to make even the smallest of decisions for them, thereby not only limiting themselves terribly, but also becoming a burden to this person. To gain the support they think they need, they may volunteer for unpleasant tasks, submit to unreasonable demands, and tolerate verbal, physical, or sexual abuse. A person who is codependent will plan their entire life around pleasing the other person—their enabler. The codependent's self-esteem and self-worth will come only from sacrificing themselves for their partner. Often, they have no personal identity, interests, or values outside of their codependent relationship. Having the ability to be happy regardless of being in a relationship is an amazing attribute. All relationships come to an end. No one is so perfect as to be irreplaceable. We can all get along with many people out there. Appreciate the time you spend with your loved ones and strive to make good memories to enjoy once they are gone from your life. Learn to stand on your own two legs. It is healthy to spend time alone, whether you are self-reflecting or simply taking part in a favorite solo activity. Take up hobbies that you enjoy on your own. Book a solo trip abroad. You may discover strength and joy you never thought you had. Committing to change is the first step to getting yourself to a healthier place.

Strive to become independent emotionally and financially—the sooner, the better. Being emotionally independent means that you can make the most of your personal decisions and go through challenging life situations without dragging other people into it unnecessarily. It can also mean less suffering and disappointment, since you do not depend on others to meet your emotional needs. Being emotionally independent will tremendously improve your personal relations with friends, family, coworkers, and other people you interact with. They will rate you more positively and will be more likely to help you on the rare occasions where you need help. When it comes to personal independence, there is no satisfaction comparable to the ability to pay your own bills. Financial independence means that you control your income and expenditure and you are not answerable to anybody. This, in turn, means that you are in control of your own life and get to draft your own destiny. Independence will give you a sense of accomplishment and power that will eventually change how you rate yourself and how others view you in the positive direction. The confidence that comes with being independent will open your mind to try out new things, learn, grow, and even take bigger risks for bigger rewards along the way. Having a free and independent mind will give you freedom to explore your skills and talents and will ultimately bring out the best in you.

Being independent does not mean, however, living in isolation or never needing help. Humans are social beings, and we have always lived in communities and relied on each other for our survival. Reciprocal exchanges are what the human social fabric is made of. The challenge in relationships is balancing togetherness and individuality. Interdependency—the healthy form of dependency—is characterized by a balance between autonomy (or the ability to function independently) and leaning on one another. An interdependent relationship allows you to give and receive help, while also retaining your individuality and autonomy. Mutual support and aid empower each individual to grow and learn. The key is being cooperative, but also assertive. Interdependent adults have a strong sense of who they are and feel competent to navigate the world and express their needs. They accept help, but do not rely on others for their self-esteem. When they are in an intimate relationship, they do not need their partner to make them whole. They are complete as individuals and complement each other as partners, meaning both partners have their individual ideas, beliefs, values, ambitions, and desires. They know and respect their differences and give each other space to pursue their interests and passions. They also confide in each other and provide mutual support when needed. Combining your expertise and efforts with those of others will result in greater outcomes for everyone. In the workplace, interdependence produces synergy, which enhances team effort beyond the simple sum total of the team members' individual skills. At the geopolitical level, it means greater cross-trading between nations. The confidence earned through increasing independence is a vital first step towards effective interdependence. It starts with being able to stand on your own, and then becoming mature enough to understand that there is even greater strength in developing a community.

Being in a position of power means one has the ability to give more than one takes. Those who constantly ask for help and are never able to pay anything back are despised for being weak. Favors are debts that need to be repaid. Do not become indebted to anyone and everyone, lest you spend your life laboring to please them. Having traded your freedom for cheap gifts, you will turn yourself into a drone. One of the most valuable resources in life is to have lots of options. Powerful people know to protect their freedom and maneuverability. They give freely, buying influence more often than things. To give is to obligate. The shrewd ones know to utilize other people's privations. They manipulate people's desires to reach their own ends. The key is to become astute in human exchanges. Nothing is ever offered for free. Rather than accepting a favor, pay for it whenever possible. By paying your own way, you can stay clear of gratitude, guilt, and deceit.

Your ability to be generous is a direct gauge of the power and influence you wield. Power and influence, in turn, will give you the ability to make a difference in the world. One can be generous in many ways, including with money, possessions, time, attention, aid, encouragement, emotional availability, knowledge, skills, talents, and more. If you have something to give that others desire, they will follow and respect you. The purpose of giving is to make others dependent on you and enhance your reputation. When there is no longer dependence, good manners and esteem quickly disappear. The key is to understand that others are primarily interested in what you can do for them. And because the human brain is intrinsically preprogrammed to return favors, if you just help enough people get what they want, you will receive anything you want back in return. Generosity is a sign of strength. Both conspicuous consumption (the ability to purchase lavish and unnecessary things) and conspicuous philanthropy (the ability to donate significant amounts of economic resources, energy, or time) can signal that an individual has excess resources. Both are meant—mostly unconsciously—to impress others and gain status. In addition to signaling wealth, public philanthropy can also convey prosocial and virtuous personality traits such as kindness, sympathy, and helpfulness. In the context of evolution, excessive spending and philanthropic displays serve to increase the signaler's status and prestige, which may ultimately increase the signaler's ability to attract and retain desirable mates. Having prosocial traits also promotes the perception that the signaler is a trustworthy exchange partner or someone whom one may preferentially want to do business with. For the wealthy, conspicuous giving may be a more effective way of garnering respect than conspicuous consumption. Indeed, the more the wealthy give their money away, the more likely it is that people will think that they are deserving of their wealth. Because people believe that rich individuals who spend their money charitably are more moral and virtuous, they view their fortunes as having been hard-earned and well-deserved. In addition, their public image of being trustworthy business partners is likely to lead to even more wealth. Their prestige will earn them friends and lovers alike. Is it any wonder that generosity activates the human brain's reward circuitry the same way that eating, drinking, and sex do? The best of it all is the fact that, regardless of why it was originally evolved and our unconsciously selfish motivations, generosity still has the fortunate side effect of actually helping others. As you build up wealth, keep your money circulating. Doing it wisely will lead to even more wealth, not less.

Avoid depending on any one person, one source of income, favor, or benefit. When it comes to essentials, the more options you have the better. Do not put all your eggs in one basket. Solely relying on employment income is doing just that—putting yourself at risk through lack of diversification. Having several income streams will make you much stronger in case of a layoff. Save as much as you can at the earliest possible age to build portfolio income and take full advantage of the power of compounding interest over time. Turn your passion or hobby into an income-generating business, whether it is by investing in rental real estate, doing freelance work, or launching your own web-based service or store. Those who say that "money cannot buy happiness" are either poor (and trying to console themselves for not having much money themselves) or wealthy beyond their wildest dreams (and trying to blend in and not look selfish). As for the highly educated social scientists who try to prove it through clever sampling, they are mainly looking for consolation from seeing those who they see as lesser beings make more money than them. Money can buy peace of mind from financial worries, options, the freedom to live your life on your own terms, great experiences, even health and beauty. It will not solve all of your problems, but it will, at the very least, allow you to wallow in your misery in some amazingly beautiful places. Accumulate wealth so that you can better navigate hardship. Have more than one best friend. Build a network of deep relationships that you can tap into for advice, help, or simply for some good time. While some of these relationships may end over time, others will endure, hedging your losses. The sharper your foresight, the more you can prepare today, the better off you will be tomorrow.

In all matters, keep something in reserve. Be generous, but do not give away all of your wealth at once. It will strip away all power, influence, and respect from you. Contrary to myth, there is no noble poverty. Esteem is directly proportional to what you can do for others. Give mindfully a little at a time while alive, and the remainder post mortem. Neither Bill Gates nor Warren Buffet will consent to give away all their wealth while alive; it would mean giving away all power. If your wealth consists of knowledge, reveal it piecewise and keep people yearning for more. How will you remain relevant if you teach it all away? Hold something back so that you can preserve your usefulness. When rewarding subordinates, leave room for further rewards. How will you motivate them to do better if you leave them fully satisfied? Preserve your superiority by keeping others dependent on you. That way, you may get applause, perhaps even a part-time consulting contract, rather than a lukewarm handshake when the time comes to wrap up your full-time career. Dignity matters, especially in old age.

15

Rule Nine: Manage Your Reputation

We all want power, and those who despise it the most vehemently are often those who want it the most ardently. Power and fame being strongly correlated, we all covet fame, admittedly or not. Fame stands for widespread reputation, especially of a favorable character, and public eminence or renown. Michel de Montaigne, the sixteenth century philosopher of the French Renaissance, said the following about fame in his *Essays:* "There is not any one of which reason so clearly accuses the vanity; but it is so deeply rooted in us that I dare not determine whether any one ever clearly discharged himself from it or no. After you have said all and believed all has been said to its prejudice, it produces so intestine an inclination in opposition to your best arguments that you have little power to resist it; for, as Cicero says, even those who most controvert it, would yet that the books they write about it should visit the light under their own names and seek to derive glory from seeming to despise it." Translated into modern English, what this means is, "Reason equates fame with vanity. But the visceral lust for fame is so powerful that, even those of us who have heard all the rational arguments against it and became convinced of them, cannot help but desire it; for, as Cicero said, even those who argue against fame still want the books they write against it to bear their name in the title and hope to become famous for despising it." Research shows that even among preadolescents, a desire to become famous for the sake of being famous is the most popular future goal. The predominant motivations for fame involve a perceived suitability and intensity for a celebrity lifestyle, namely the desire to be seen and valued publicly, living a life of wealth, helping family and friends financially, and being a role model for others. When you are famous, your good reputation precedes you. Total strangers admire you and smile at you because your merits have been impressively explained in advance. Fame means that other people will be flattered and delighted to be in your company, even if you are only slightly interested in them. Furthermore, no one will be able to afford to upset you. Your complaints will be taken seriously and your happiness will become the focus of everyone's efforts. You will have the power to make or break other people's reputations. Your high status alone can intimidate enough to secure victory, sparing you the trouble of waging a war. Doors will be held open to you, while kept shut for many. Celebrity means referent power, and referent power means unimaginable wealth through generous endorsement contracts for commercial products and services. Having wealth means that you will live in beautiful places, receive the best treatment and services, have options that most people can only dream of, and have the ability to be generous to the people and causes that matter to you. While fame has clear advantages, it can present serious disadvantages as well, especially when poorly managed. One obvious disadvantage is the loss of privacy that comes with it. Another one is that being famous can seriously upset others. The celebrity of a few people will always contrast painfully with the obscurity of the many. If you are one of the few lucky people to attain celebrity status, be careful not to become the target of the resentment of the many who feel slighted and neglected by an unfair world. Fame will throw you open to unlimited judgement and schadenfreude. Manage your reputation with the utmost care. You built it with your talent, sweat, and toil—now guard it zealously. You owe it to your past self. Avoid acting like a snotty diva just because you are now famous. Respect others and be kind. Conspicuous generosity is, perhaps, the best antidote for the occasional cruel attacks on a celebrity's character or merit. Being publicly generous will promote the belief that you are a trustworthy individual whose wealth is based on merit. By giving back to those who have elevated you, you can have your fame and fortune and, even more importantly, enjoy them as well.

Do not be chained to the status quo by limitations in your mind. The tale of the elephant and the rope powerfully illustrates how repeated rebuffs and failures in our past may erect mental barriers that only become higher and sturdier over time and keep us from reaching our full potential. As the tale goes, two friends were passing by an adult elephant held by only a thin rope tied to one of its front legs. Despite the obvious fact that this huge and powerful animal could easily uproot a tree or smash a human being to pulp in a split-second, it did nothing to break away from the weak rope it was tied to. They decided to ask the trainer nearby why the animal made no attempt to get away.

"Well," the trainer replied, "it has been tied with the same rope from an earlier age where the rope was enough to restrain it physically. As it grew up, it became conditioned to believe that it was impossible to break free. So it never even tries."

Learned helplessness can make us expect loss without even trying. Self-imposed limitations can prevent us from achieving our best in our career, relationships, and goals. It is a human tendency to spin up assumptions to fill in missing information regarding a situation or a person, and then to become convinced that what we just made up must be the truth. When applied to ourselves, the assumptions we make up tend to follow accepted norms or past experience and can represent a tremendous opportunity cost by limiting our thought, creativity, and potential for innovation. Do not be the elephant tied up by an invisible rope. Check the facts. You may not necessarily win if you try, but if you do not try, all you will have is the status quo. Dream big to achieve big. Greatness is what brings renown.

People will treat you in exact proportion to the way you carry yourself. Things often pass for what they appear to be, not for what they may be in actuality. Most people will judge you based solely on appearances, never probing deeper than the surface. You are worth the price you name. Appearing vulnerable will make others despise you. If you exude confidence instead, they will respect you without consciously knowing why. Nietzsche wrote, "With all great deceivers there is a noteworthy occurrence to which they owe their power. In the actual act of deception they are overcome by belief in themselves. It is this which then speaks so miraculously and compellingly to those who surround them." All great deceivers may have been blessed with a narcissistic personality, evolved to instill in those possessing it the unshakeable belief in their unconditional superiority over everyone else. Coupled with talent and favorable circumstance, this belief, however delusional, may actually lead to a place of superiority over others. So polish the facade you put up in front of others. Keep your head up, your back straight, and your posture open. Dress pleasantly and appropriately. Make eye contact. Speak courteously, but assertively. The key is to radiate confidence, not arrogance or disdain. Believe firmly in your own greatness, and it may well become a self-fulfilling prophecy.

Our reputations represent the way others perceive us. A good reputation can open doors to opportunities, friendships, and jobs. It can even come to your rescue from malevolence when others spontaneously rise to your defense without even knowing it. It is hard to have friends if people think you are mean-spirited and hard to make a living in any capacity if people think you are lazy, unreliable, or dishonest. In business, your reputation is everything since referrals and recommendations can make or break a company. Developing a good reputation takes time, consistency, and patience. Destroying a good reputation, in contrast, only requires a single moment's misstep. Warren Buffet has succinctly summed it up: "It takes twenty years to build a reputation and five minutes to ruin it. If you think about that, you will do things differently." If you live up to your reputation most of the time, but fail to do so on a rare instance, you risk disproportionate damage if the person you let down is highly influential in your network. The key to building a good reputation is taking consistent action that embodies the characteristics you want others to associate with you. Underpinning much of our success is the compounding effect of the small daily or weekly decisions and actions that we take. You cannot establish a track record by constantly shifting gears. If you are known to consistently follow through on your promises, people will appreciate that and remember you for it. Overpromising, overextending, and overestimating will cast a shadow on your character. Be genuine, trustworthy, and loyal. Give credit where credit is due. Speak well and act even better. Reputation is a powerful cognitive shortcut in the minds of others. It is difficult to build, easy to lose, and requires constant attention and care to remain effective and credible over time. When your behaviors reflect your values, words, and promises, people will know and trust what to expect from you. Consistency is paramount to managing perceptions, preventing confusion, and increasing trust. It starts with closing the gaps between what you say and what you do.

In today's digital environment, it does not take gross misconduct to damage your personal reputation or that of your brand's. A misunderstanding, honest mistake, or snappy online reply to an angry person can do significant harm. Thanks to the widespread use of social media, information can truly travel at the speed of light. If you are the owner of a business or a brand, it is imperative that you maintain full control over your social media presence. Even if you do not plan on being active on all social media channels, you should take steps to create accounts so that you are the owner of all accounts associated with your name and the name of your business or brand. Squatters can open social media accounts bearing your name or the name of your business and demand a hefty sum to sell them to you. It can take time to get these accounts closed down, giving the fraudsters ample opportunity to do substantial damage to your reputation. If you do have a social media presence, do not use these platforms as your personal space for airing your dirty laundry. CEOs and other executives have lost positions or had to do significant damage control due to poor behavior, misunderstandings, and a lack of appropriate response during a crisis. Remember that everything you post online will live on the internet forever, open to everyone's view, including that of prospective employers, customers, or clients. Remain polite and professional at all times. If you go online and find a review that is not just negative, but dishonest and vulgar, take some time to calm down, then respond politely and matter-of-factly. It is a good practice to set up digital alerts to learn about stories mentioning you or your business. This way, if some news breaks that should concern you, you will know about it sooner rather than later. By responding in a timely manner, you can control how things unfold. If you happen to have done something wrong, the best step forward is to take ownership of the offense and offer some corrective action. Cancer always starts with just one cell. If you let it propagate, it will overtake your entire body and, eventually, leave you dead. Managing damage to your online image is much like managing cancer—the sooner you detect it and intervene, the better. Manage your online presence proactively by paying attention to news about your company and yourself, responding appropriately to problems, maintaining dignity and poise at all times, and exercising full control over your online presence.

Do your best to repair your reputation, should it get tainted. A bad reputation can ruin your career, damage your relationships, cost you opportunities, deal a serious blow to your self-confidence, and even cause legal or financial troubles. Before taking any action, assess the situation to get a clear picture of how serious the damage is, which areas of your life have been affected, and the role you may have played. Better than doing this alone and in the heat of emotions, ask for the neutral view of a trusted friend or colleague. Get professional advice if the issue at hand has legal ramifications. A bystander's objective point of view can offer a balanced perspective on your personality and the issue at hand, as well as constructive advice for moving forward. Use your assessment and the external feedback to create a plan for damage control. If the problems at hand are complex and clearly outside of your expertise, hire the best professional help you can get to solve them. If your reputation has been sullied due to malevolent gossip, it is important to approach the people who have been spreading the lies, clarify the facts, and ask that they stop. Then explain the situation to the other people who have been affected with the rumors. Do this as quickly as possible to prevent a bad situation from becoming worse by letting people's imaginations run wild. If the blemished reputation is your own fault, begin to repair the damage by owning up to your behavior and making amends to anyone you have wronged. Admit your mistakes, apologize, and offer a way to make things right. With the initial hard work of honesty and communication out of the way, start the next phase of the damage control by doing good deeds. Give compliments. Help others. Donate to charity. Keep your head down, honor your promises, and work hard. Do it consistently over an extended time period and, with luck, others will take notice of your sincere efforts to grow and reevaluate their view of you as a result.

Do not get trapped into doing someone else's dirty work. It is an old trick used by politicians and other powerful people everywhere. It consists of finding a scapegoat to take the blame for them when things go awfully bad or when a heinous act needs to be done in order to get a personal benefit. By utilizing others to receive the blame for their actions or circumstances, they shift public attention from their own shortcomings and avert anything that might incite misgivings towards their position or potency. The scapegoat is usually a close friend who is perceived to be relatively weak. This trick is best illustrated by the fable of the monkey and the cat. As the fable goes, a monkey and a cat were pets in the same household and were great friends. One day they were sitting by the fire, watching some chestnuts roasting on the hearth. The cunning monkey immediately thought of using flattery to induce the cat to pull the chestnuts out of the fire. The cat took the bait and started to pull the burning chestnuts one by one, each time singeing her paw severely. Not only did the monkey eat all the chestnuts the cat pulled out, but it took none of the blame from their owner who only saw the missing chestnuts and the cat's burnt paw. Just as the monkey lost a close friend forever, the person using this trick runs the serious risk of losing friends, followers, and much more. Deceit is rampant and the best defense against guile is attentiveness. But if you find yourself in the position of the scapegoat, you may have coercive leverage over the bully. Expose them, and they will lose the thing they feared losing most: their untarnished reputation.

Head off rumors. The higher your social standing, the higher your likelihood of becoming the target of blackmail. The attack on your reputation can come from those whom you least suspect of betrayal—your friends, trusted coworkers, even your relatives. The ensuing public warfare can leave you emotionally and financially drained. If you think someone is spreading untruths about you, you need to react quickly to stop them. The only fight you are guaranteed to lose is the one you back down from. Sit down and speak frankly with the person you believe is creating the rumors.

The best defense is, however, preemptive. Never tell others—no matter how close—your biggest weaknesses, because those are things that can be used against you in the future. Your defects give others power over you. This is especially true in work relationships, where rivalry and envy are common. There is no quicker way to hurt your career—particularly in niche professions, where a lot of people know each other—than to allow rumors to circulate about you. Not knowing how to hide a one-off mistake is to err twice. Resist the temptation to share your sorrow when it hurts. What weakens us is exactly where malice will pounce. If you must entrust your honor into someone else's hand, make sure you have theirs in pledge. It will give you leverage against betrayal. Watch out for deceit, but do it subtly so as not lose other people's trust. When it comes to reputation management, an ounce of prevention is worth a pound of cure.

Good reputation management is as much about form as it is about substance. If you are in a position of power, administer rewards yourself and in public view—but punishments should be meted out through others and behind the scenes. When something pleases others, do it yourself—when it displeases, delegate it. You will win acclaim and shift blame onto others. As every management consultant will tell you, a decision to downsize is always made by corporate executives beforehand, and the consultants are only hired to be the bearers of bad news. A bitter pill is best delivered with a generous coating of sugar. Inform yourself as much as possible about a situation before judging the appropriate course of action. Being accurately informed will allow you to bring about better consequences. And the better the outcome of your actions, the more favorably you will be judged. The higher your status, the more stringent the public scrutiny. So speak well and act even better.

When you start something, do not raise other people's expectations un-necessarily. Imagination always travels much further than reality and, most of the time, leads straight to disappointment. It is better to underpromise and overdeliver. When reality surpasses expectations, people will be left wondering what more you are capable of. Avoid speaking in superlatives. Exaggeration, especially the excessive kind, is a form of lying. It will cast a shadow not only on your character, but also on your ability to make judgements. Do it more than once and you will lose all respect. Some people are all facade, looking like a mansion from the outside, but empty and unfinished from the inside. They are all about words, never deeds. The sharp-sighted, who know to look deeper than the bark, can spot them at once and steer clear of them. Walk the talk, and an extra mile. Learn from the good merchants of Louisiana who are always keen on delighting their customers by adding a lagniappe to their purchase—something they throw in, gratis, for good measure, like a thirteenth roll on a baker's dozen. Deliver what you promised and add a little more. It will delight others and do wonders for your reputation.

16

Rule Ten: Be Adaptable

Sharpen your foresight. Foresight is the uniquely human ability to see what is likely to happen in the future and take appropriate action. People who can think ahead will be prepared to take advantage of all the new opportunities that rapid social and technological progress are creating, avoiding problems that trap other people. Indeed, students lacking foresight are more likely to neglect their studies because they fail to see the connection between education and future success. Young people who do not learn to think ahead may find it difficult to plan for a successful marriage and family life. People whose foresight is weak are likely to have difficulty saving money for emergencies or for future financial needs, such as paying for their children's college education, retirement, or long-term care. In a world that is changing at a faster pace than ever, foresight gives us increased power to shape our futures. People in business can use foresight to identify new products, services, and markets. Foresight may reveal potential threats that we can prepare to deal with before they become crises. It can motivate us to take care of our precious health so that we may live well now and in old age. Foresight relies on memories and past experiences to imagine future events. This is because we use our past experiences as a way to learn general rules or guidelines on how the world really works. We then take these guidelines and use them to predict future events. A good way to improve foresight is, therefore, to live a life full of meaningful experiences. This means doing new things, taking risks, and learning from failures. Given how short our lives are, reading is essential to capitalize on the experiences of others so that we do not have to reinvent the wheel. As you read, do not just memorize. Rather, try to understand the cause-and-effect relationships behind each statement. Always be willing to test your assumptions with a critical eye. Keep yourself informed about current events and new technology and use that knowledge to envision scenarios about how the future might unfold. Since past events are not always good predictors of what the future may hold, your foresight will never be perfect. But the more accurately you can imagine what the future is likely to bring, the better positioned you will be to reap the benefits from that future reality.

John F. Kennedy said, "Change is the law of life. And those who look only to the past or the present are certain to miss the future." Adapting to change requires a high level of flexibility. Without it, you will find yourself wanting or needing things to go a certain way, wishing things were different, and struggling to deal with the challenges that come your way. Your ability to adapt can increase your chances of being successful in your career, relationships, health, and more. All growth occurs outside of our comfort zones. It is also where creativity and innovation live. Become as skilled at detecting and riding out popular trends as professional surfers are at catching the most powerful waves. It requires that you be patient and learn to stand back when the time is not yet ripe, ready to act quickly when the right moment strikes. Those who miss the necessity to evolve risk becoming personally and professionally obsolete. The choice is yours—you can either bury your head in the sand or look out onto the horizon and sail to new lands. If you are an employee, you chair your own enterprise and loan your talents to companies that pay you. You are responsible for your career, not your employers. Make sure you follow the trends in your profession and keep your skills up to date so that you can remain relevant. Businesses that fail to adjust their value propositions to the changing needs of consumers risk failing. We live in a world that loves everything new and, to stay relevant, you need to be coming up with new products and services constantly. What this means for business leaders is that learning to manage change effectively is more important than ever. If you are new to a position of power or an outsider trying to build a power base, preach the need for change, but be sure to respect the old way of doing things by reforming in small steps. While innovation can only happen as a result of change, too much change at once can leave people traumatized and trigger revolt. Float a trial balloon to see how well something is accepted and received, especially when you doubt its popularity or success. Life does not stop unfolding just because we come up against an obstacle. So get inventive with what you already have around you and adapt to your situation. The key to adapting and overcoming is to make a plan and follow through. The plan may have to be revised as circumstances change, but having a plan of action will give you direction, meaning, and purpose. The mountain you need to climb will become a little smaller with time and, before you know it, the plan will be achieved.

Adapt yourself to the prevailing zeitgeist—the schema of fashions and fads that make up what is considered to be tasteful, appropriate, or popular at any given time. Eminence is a strong function of zeitgeist and, like all other things, it too goes in and out of fashion. Leaders emerge when the mix of their personality traits happens to be matched with the prevailing preferences particularly well, or when their abilities and skills are suited particularly well to those needed in nascent industries. Some talent always goes to waste as a result of being ill-suited to the times. Some people have the right traits, but fail to take advantage of them. Some greatness is only recognized by posterity. For instance, although each of Van Gogh's paintings sell for tens of millions of dollars today, he died unknown and poor. Go with the prevailing tide. Act mad when madness prevails and keep wisdom for private company. Being a hypocrite is sometimes a necessity. When the public at large has chosen to follow an absurd custom, pretend to follow it too, lest you become scorned and marginalized, if not brutalized. Most human decisions are made based on emotion and justified post hoc with logic. Large swaths of people have been known to go mad together—for a salient example, consider the Germans and their conspirators in genocide during World War II. Observe people's temperaments and intelligence and adapt yourself accordingly. Where ignorance reigns, keep your knowledge hidden, lest you be deemed arrogant, condescending, or something worse. Similarity is the basis of friendships and partnerships alike. Uniqueness is originality attributed to a single person, who often simply joined an emerging undercurrent and went on to lead it. All fashions have their season and, like most things in life, they too shall eventually pass away. Take advantage of novelty while it pleases the masses. If you decide to take up residence in a new state or country, follow the conventions of the people around you. When in Rome, it is advisable to do as the Romans do.

Quit while you are ahead and, like Bill Gates or Oprah Winfrey, you can leave a sterling reputation as you move on. Fortune only shines for so long. All the good poker players know that. Celebrity is as ephemeral as it is rare. Cash in and run before things inevitably crash and burn. It is a phenomenon we see time and again, particularly with high-profile celebrities, musicians, and athletes, who believe that their careers are eternal before falling from grace because they run out of steam. Knowing when to gracefully make your exit in situations like this can be tough, since their positive nature can easily cloud your judgment. Use the time after beating a personal best for reflection to recalibrate what a personal best really means to you. If your competitive fire is still burning and you think that it is realistically possible to perform at the same level or better for a while longer, keep enjoying the incredible rush that comes with being at your acme. When you have set yourself a particularly challenging goal and worked hard to achieve it, however, motivation is likely to go down. It is wiser to retire a racehorse rather than to wait for it to collapse in the middle of a race. It will be remembered for its glory rather than disgrace. Likewise, you may want to end on a high note rather than being remembered as a failure after working so hard to win. If you are an entrepreneur, putting your business up for sale while it is on top might be the wisest entrepreneurial move you ever make. Leading a company through the various stages of its life cycle requires skills you may not have. It may be best to step back and let someone else's talent and ambition take what you started to a higher level. Few can replicate the career tracks of Warren Buffett and Rupert Murdoch, white-haired prodigies who have no need to ever call it quits. Leaving on top by exiting gracefully begins with recognizing that a job, like a life stage or a relationship, has peaked. The transition to what is next may take a while. Live life incrementally. Break your departure into manageable steps. By carefully staging your exit, you will build confidence for the next chapter of your life.

Keep reinventing yourself. Do not become shackled to the past. Push your comfort zone. Strike out anew while you are still hardy enough to face new challenges. The best way to do this is to capitalize on your prior experiences. Vera Wang, for instance, started out as a figure skater. When she failed to qualify for the 1968 US Olympic team, she knew she had to reinvent herself. She transitioned into journalism and worked as a fashion editor for *Vogue* for a decade and a half, and then reinvented herself again by becoming a design director for Ralph Lauren. She leveraged the skills she gained there into designing her own wedding dress, then opened a bridal boutique, and launched her own signature collection. Hugely popular well into the seventh decade of her life, she has a large Hollywood following at the time of this writing, and also designs lingerie, jewelry, and home products. Wang not only left each life stage at the top of her game, she parlayed each of her winnings into even greater success at the next life stage. For her, like for anyone else launching their own business or venturing out into a new career path, life offers no guarantee of success. Failure is highly likely. Starting a business will take up every minute of your life, drain all of your energy, put immense stress on your shoulders, and often pay you little to no return in terms of either money or recognition for many years. It can take herculean strength and courage to reinvent yourself by starting over after having put all that work to succeed into your first or second path. If you stop learning and stop challenging yourself, however, all you will do is vegetate—and ultimately slide into a slow death. An unused muscle is quick to atrophy. So renew yourself. Be reborn with each new challenge. There is no need to die before your time is up.

Some people seem to be born with a happier, more carefree disposition than others, and research does indicate that some of our propensity for resilience and sense of well-being may be in our genes—but only partly. More than half of happiness stems from life satisfaction, the feeling of being engaged in everyday activities and the feeling of having a purpose in life. The more positive you feel about your past and present, the more optimistic you are likely to be about the future, and the likelier you are to be satisfied with your life in general. Learn to see the glass half-full and find consolation in everything. All dark clouds come with a silver lining. All things have pros and cons. Circumstances look different when seen in a different light. Look at the world through the lens of happiness rather than sorrow. Leave the door open for friends to go away and for enemies to come through. To live well, let live. Be peaceable and practical. It is not good enough to have extraordinary knowledge—it is just as important to be versed in ordinary necessities. Living well is also about being able to connect with the people around us and feel engaged at work, in our relationships, and during our leisure time. Physical activity is not just helpful for your body, it is also great for your mind. Nothing can lift mood like the feel-good endorphins released during exercise. Keep your diet healthy, sleep well, and show kindness to those around you. Choose your line of work with care, in line with your genetic self, and work hard. But also play hard. Embrace the hardship that comes with achieving your goals. Be sure to celebrate each milestone on the way there. Take time off to travel, connect with nature, and engage in fun activities. Having meaning and purpose in life results from the feeling that what you do in life is not done in vain, that it truly matters, and that it makes a positive difference in the world. The best talent to be endowed with is the ability to quickly size up what matters. Too much life is wasted on trivialities—mechanical tasks that take much time and yield little value. Meanwhile many worthy endeavors are never even attempted. Take risks, dare to fail, then pick yourself back up and fight some more. Emigrate to another country if your character and abilities could find more fertile ground elsewhere than in your native land. Tastes are as varied as are people themselves. No matter what you do, there will be people to condemn it and others to appreciate it. Life is both trivial and profoundly serious. Have a sense of humor. You cannot control everything. Circumstances matter. Luck grants us success only rarely. Do not become despondent. Leave room for better things in your future. In the theater of life, live well and be careful to end even better.

REFERENCES

Anderson, Cameron, and Gavin J. Kilduff. "The Pursuit of Status in Social Groups." *Current Directions in Psychological Science* 18, no. 5 (2009): 295-298.

Aristotle. *Nicomachean Ethics.* United Kingdom: Penguin Classics, 2004.

Beaver, Kevin M., John Paul Wright, Brian B. Boutwell, J. C. Barnes, Matt DeLisi, and Michael G. Vaughn. "Exploring the Association Between the 2-Repeat Allele of the MAOA Gene Promoter Polymorphism and Psychopathic Personality Traits, Arrests, Incarceration, and Lifetime Antisocial Behavior." *Personality and Individual Differences* 54, no. 2 (2013): 164-168.

Churchill, Winston. *Churchill by Himself: The Definitive Collection of Quotations.* United States: PublicAffairs, 2008.

Cialdini, Robert B. *Influence: The Psychology of Persuasion.* United States: Harper Business, 2006.

DeScioli, Peter, and Robert Kurzban. "A Solution to the Mysteries of Morality." *Psychological Bulletin* 139, no. 2 (2013): 477-496.

Duckworth, Angela L., Christopher Peterson, Michael D. Matthews, and Dennis R. Kelly. "Grit: Perseverance and Passion for Long-Term Goals." *Journal of Personality and Social Psychology* 92, no. 6 (2007): 1087–1101.

English, Micaela, and Katie Robinson. "The Best Oscar Wilde Quotes." *Town and Country Magazine*, October 16, 2017.

Flynn, Francis J., Ray E. Reagans, Emily T. Amanatullah, and Daniel R. Ames. "Helping One's Way to the Top: Self-Monitors Achieve Status by Helping Others and Knowing Who Helps Whom." *Journal of Personality and Social Psychology* 91, no. 6 (2006): 1123-1137.

Franklin, Benjamin. *The Autobiography of Benjamin Franklin*. United States: Chartwell Books, 2015.

French, John R. P., Jr., and Bertram Raven. *The Bases of Social Power*. In D. Cartwright (3rd Ed.), *Group Dynamics: Research and Theory*. New York: Harper & Row, 1968.

Freud, Sigmund. *Introductory Lectures on Psychoanalysis*. United States: Liveright, 1989.

Frydman, Cary, Colin Farrell Camerer, Peter Bossaerts, and Antonio Rangel. "MAOA-L Carriers Are Better at Making Optimal Financial Decisions Under Risk." *Proceedings of the Royal Society B: Biological Sciences* 278, no. 1714 (2010): 2053-2059.

Gracián, Baltasar. *The Art of Worldly Wisdom: A Pocket Oracle*. United States: Doubleday, 1992.

Greene, Robert. *The 48 Laws of Power*. United States: Penguin Books, 2000.

Halevy, Nir, Eileen Y. Chou, and Adam D. Galinsky. "A Functional Model of Hierarchy: Why, How, and When Vertical Differentiation Enhances Group Performance." *Organizational Psychology Review* 1, no. 1 (2011): 32-52.

Hardy, Charlie L., and Mark Van Vugt. "Nice Guys Finish First: The Competitive Altruism Hypothesis." *Personality and Social Psychology Bulletin* 32, no. 10 (2006): 1402–1413.

Hobbes, Thomas. *Leviathan*. Dover Ed. United States: Dover Publications, 2006.

Jonason, Peter K., and Laura Krause. "The Emotional Deficits Associated with the Dark Triad Traits: Cognitive Empathy, Affective Empathy, and Alexithymia." *Personality and Individual Differences* 55, no. 5 (2013): 532–537.

Johnson, Andrew, and Andy McSmith. "Children Say Being Famous Is Best Thing in World." *The Independent*, December 18, 2006 at 1:00 p.m. GMT.

Keltner, Dacher, Deborah H. Gruenfeld, and Cameron Anderson. "Power, Approach, and Inhibition." *Psychological Review* 110, no. 2 (2003): 265-284.

Koski, Jessica, Hongling Xie, and Ingrid R. Olson. "Understanding Social Hierarchies: The Neural and Psychological Foundations of Status Perception." *Social Neuroscience* 10, no. 5 (2015): 527-550.

La Bruyère, Jean de. *The "Characters" of Jean de La Bruyère*. London: John C. Nimmo, 1885.

Machiavelli, Niccolò. *The Discourses on the First Ten Books of Titus Livy*. United Kingdom: Penguin Books, 1974.

Machiavelli, Niccolò. *The Prince*. Canada: Prohyptikon Publishing Inc., 2009.

Madsen, Douglas. "A Biochemical Property Relating to Power Seeking in Humans." *American Political Science Review* 79, no. 2 (1985): 448-457.

Madsen, Douglas. "Power Seekers Are Different: Further Biochemical Evidence." *American Political Science Review* 80, no. 1 (1986): 261-270.

Marx, Karl. *Critique of Hegel's "Philosophy of Right."* United Kingdom:

Cambridge University Press, 2009.

Mathieu, Cynthia, and Étienne St-Jean. "Entrepreneurial Personality: The Role of Narcissism." *Personality and Individual Differences* 55, no. 5 (2013): 527-531.

McDermott, Rose, Chris Dawes, Elizabeth Prom-Wormley, Lindon Eaves, and Peter K. Hatemi. "MAOA and Aggression: A Gene–Environment Interaction in Two Populations." *Journal of Conflict Resolution* 57, no. 6 (2012): 1043-1064.

Mikhail, John. "Universal Moral Grammar: Theory, Evidence and the Future." *Trends in Cognitive Sciences* 11, no. 4 (2007): 143–152.

Milgram, Stanley. "Behavioral Study of Obedience." *Journal of Abnormal and Social Psychology* 67, no. 4 (1963): 371-378.

Montaigne, Michel de. *Essays of Montaigne, vol.* 3. Trans. Charles Cotton, revised by William Carew Hazlett. New York: Edwin C. Hill, 1910.

Nietzsche, Friedrich. *Beyond Good and Evil.* United Kingdom: Penguin Classics, 2003.

Nietzsche, Friedrich. *Human, All Too Human.* United States: Prometheus Books, 2009.

Nietzsche, Friedrich. *The Will to Power.* United Kingdom: Penguin Classics, 2017.

Osorio, Carlos, Thomas Probert, Edgar Jones, Allan H. Young, and Ian Robbins. "Adapting to Stress: Understanding the Neurobiology of Resilience." *Behavioral Medicine* 43, no. 4 (2017): 307-322.

Pediaditakis, Nicholas. "The Association Between Major Mental Disorders and Geniuses." *Psychiatric Times* 31, no. 9 (2014): 1-4.

Rousseau, Jean-Jacques. *Émile: Or On Education*. United States: Basic Books, 1979.

Seery, Mark D., E. Alison Holman, and Roxane Cohen Silver. "Whatever Does Not Kill Us: Cumulative Lifetime Adversity, Vulnerability, and Resilience." *Journal of Personality and Social Psychology* 99, no. 6 (2010): 1025–1041.

Shaftesbury, Anthony Ashley Cooper, The Third Earl of. *Soliloquy: Or, Advice to an Author*. United States: Creative Media Partners, LLC, 2018.

Shamay-Tsoory, Simone G., Judith Aharon-Peretz, and Daniella Perry. "Two Systems for Empathy: A Double Dissociation Between Emotional and Cognitive Empathy in Inferior Frontal Gyrus Versus Ventromedial Prefrontal Lesions." *Brain* 132, no. 3 (2009): 617-627.

Simmons, Gene. *On Power: My Journey Through the Corridors of Power and How You Can Get More Power*. United States: Dey Street Books, 2017.

Snyder, Benjamin. "7 Insights from Legendary Investor Warren Buffett." *CNBC*, May 1, 2017 at 4:26 p.m. EDT.

Spurk, Daniel, Anita C. Keller, and Andreas Hirschi. "Do Bad Guys Get Ahead or Fall Behind? Relationships of the Dark Triad of Personality with Objective and Subjective Career Success." *Social Psychological and Personality Science* 7, no. 2 (2016): 113-121.

Talzoya. *Of Lovers, Lonely Hearts, and the Psychotic Spell Called Falling in Love*. United States: Voltis Press, 2020.

Twain, Mark. "What Paul Bourget Thinks of Us." *The North American Review*

160, no. 458 (1895): 48-62.

Weeden, Jason, Adam B. Cohen, and Douglas T. Kenrick. "Religious Attendance as Reproductive Support." *Evolutionary Human Behavior* 29, no. 5 (2008): 327-334.

Whatley, Mark A., J. Matthew Webster, Richard H. Smith, and Adele Rhodes. "The Effect of a Favor on Public and Private Compliance: How Internalized is the Norm of Reciprocity?" *Basic and Applied Social Psychology* 21, no. 3 (1999): 251–259.

Made in the USA
Coppell, TX
30 September 2021

63257377R00098

"The supreme power in the country belongs to the people." (1932)

"I had no desire to change from one king to many—which is a democratic system but only its outer husk. I am focused on the important point: 'improve the well-being of the people'." (1933)

"Freedom does not mean that a person can do anything he likes. That would become anarchy, the lack of any government. Freedom must have rules. Freedom must exist within the scope of law and morality." (1934)

". . . the slavery vision is a danger to the Thai nation and people. Sooner or later it provides the support for dictators to return with increased power and again govern the people as slaves. The dictator changes from person to person, but the dictatorship remains." (1973)

"The party or revolutionary movement to establish a new society is thus comprised of people who were born in the old society. They . . . forsake their standing in the old system and devote their lives to establish a progressive new society. But . . . they carry the residual vision and habits of the old society embedded within themselves. There are differences in the degree to which different people can abandon these old traces." (1982)